Learn Red – Fundamentals of Red

Get up and running with the Red language for full-stack development

Ivo Balbaert

BIRMINGHAM - MUMBAI

Learn Red – Fundamentals of Red

Commissioning Editor: Richa Tripathi
Acquisition Editor: Denim Pinto
Content Development Editor: Akshada Iyer
Technical Editor: Abhishek Sharma
Copy Editor: Safis Editing
Project Coordinator: Prajakta Naik
Proofreader: Safis Editing
Indexer: Tejal Daruwale Soni
Graphics: Jisha Chirayil
Production Coordinator: Shraddha Falebhai

First published: May 2018

Production reference: 1170518

Published by Packt Publishing Ltd.
Livery Place
35 Livery Street
Birmingham
B3 2PB, UK.

ISBN 978-1-78913-070-6

www.packtpub.com

To my wife, Christiane, for the loving support during the writing of this book

`mapt.io`

Mapt is an online digital library that gives you full access to over 5,000 books and videos, as well as industry leading tools to help you plan your personal development and advance your career. For more information, please visit our website.

Why subscribe?

- Spend less time learning and more time coding with practical eBooks and Videos from over 4,000 industry professionals

- Improve your learning with Skill Plans built especially for you

- Get a free eBook or video every month

- Mapt is fully searchable

- Copy and paste, print, and bookmark content

PacktPub.com

Did you know that Packt offers eBook versions of every book published, with PDF and ePub files available? You can upgrade to the eBook version at `www.PacktPub.com` and as a print book customer, you are entitled to a discount on the eBook copy. Get in touch with us at `service@packtpub.com` for more details.

At `www.PacktPub.com`, you can also read a collection of free technical articles, sign up for a range of free newsletters, and receive exclusive discounts and offers on Packt books and eBooks.

Foreword

When a new language is created, programmers and technology pundits are quick to ask "Why?," whether it's a programming, markup, or modeling language. Designers are often criticized, rather than praised, as if looking for new and better approaches is a bad thing. The critics couldn't be more wrong. That doesn't mean every new tool or idea will succeed, in theory or in practice. However, we must keep trying, if we hope to move forward or even keep pace. The world isn't standing still, and neither can we. As a conservative technologist (nee Luddite), I have to be reminded of this from time to time.

When an author, in this day and age, writes a book about technology, others are quick to ask "Why? Isn't everything you need to know available on the internet?." Sure, if you know where to look, are able to separate the wheat from the chaff (Luddites love time-tested idioms), and your noble goal is to work from original sources. If, however, you're a programmer in 2018, you may not have the luxury and time for pure research about every new technology that comes along, at an ever-increasing pace.

At this point, you're looking for a TL;DR (Too Long; Didn't Read), right? You're three paragraphs in, and already feeling pressured to move on. Your time is valuable and isn't to be wasted. I couldn't agree more. That's why you should read this book. It is a TL;DR for the Red language, and the Red language is your TL;DR for software development.

If you've never heard of Red, you don't know what makes it special, how to use it, or what it's capable of. This book will show you. It's not a primer or a technical manual; it's an introduction. It's your friend Ivo, waving you over at a cocktail party and saying "Hey, this is Red. I think you two might get along. Red is..." and runs down Red's C.V. while throwing in a few saucy details to pique your interest.

The more you talk to Red, the more it opens your mind to new ways of thinking. That's your job, remember? Thinking and solving problems. Writing code is, or should be, incidental. Sadly, the complexity of modern software development has turned things upside down, while simultaneously sucking the fun out of making software. Red wants to change that, and this book will help you get started.

Red will seem familiar, but also strange. It's approachable, but technically advanced. There's nothing quite like it (except its predecessor, Rebol, of course). One minute you're using it as a scripting language, the next it's cross-compiling your reactive GUI application, from your current environment, with C-level speed extensions, into stand-alone executables, each about 1 MB in size. You look like a superhero, but your sidekick is the one doing all the work.

Or maybe you thought we don't need any new languages.

Gregg Irwin

Red Community Manager
Head of the Operational Team of the Red Language Foundation

Contributors

About the author

Ivo Balbaert is a former lecturer for (Web) programming and databases at CVO Antwerpen, a community college in Belgium. He received a PhD in applied physics from the University of Antwerp in 1986. He worked for 20 years in the software industry as a developer and consultant in several companies, and for 10 years as a project manager at the University Hospital of Antwerp. Since 2000, he has been partly teaching, developing software, and writing technical books, among others:

- *Rust Essentials*
- *Getting Started with Julia*
- *The Way to Go*

I would especially like to thank my reviewer, Rudolf Meijer, who clarified many things and made this book so much better and more accurate. Also, my gratitude to the many experts in the Red community, especially Mike Parr, Nick Antonaccio, and André Ungaretti, and above all, the deepest admiration for Nenad Rakocevic, the creator of Red, and Carl Sassenrath, who started it all with Rebol.

About the reviewer

Rudolf Meijer wrote his first computer program in 1966. He was involved in the creation and formal definition of several programming languages, notably CHILL and Ada. He has programmed in Fortran II and IV, COBOL, Turbo Pascal, Visual Basic, Euphoria, Rebol, and now Red. He has contributed to the development of Rebol and is now strongly involved with Red, having published a formal specification of Red/System and preparing one for Red itself.

Packt is searching for authors like you

If you're interested in becoming an author for Packt, please visit `authors.packtpub.com` and apply today. We have worked with thousands of developers and tech professionals, just like you, to help them share their insight with the global tech community. You can make a general application, apply for a specific hot topic that we are recruiting an author for, or submit your own idea.

Table of Contents

Preface

This book is about the Red programming language and environment. It highlights its specific features, such as its compactness and full-stack capabilities. Red is different from other languages. It approaches programming differently and perhaps doesn't have all the shiny things from most mainstream languages that you come to expect. Rather, it gives you better tools for thought and for getting your job done. This book will give you a head start with this new inspiring technology.

The book is ready for the 0.6.4 version. All code examples have been tested under this release.

Who this book is for

This book is aimed at software developers and architects who want to learn Red because of its conciseness, flexibility, expressiveness, and more specifically, for its possibilities in GUI apps and blockchain/smart contract programming. Some knowledge of the basic concepts and experience of any programming language is assumed.

What this book covers

Chapter 1, *Red's Mission*, talks about the main characteristics of Red and motivates the reader to embark on their Red journey.

Chapter 2, *Setting Up for Development*, teaches the reader how to install Red on their system and start working with the Red console and with code files in a development environment.

Chapter 3, *Using Words, Values, and Types*, takes a look at the basic building blocks of a Red program—words and values. We discuss the different types available in Red.

Chapter 4, *Code-Controlling Structures*, focuses on how blocks, values, and words are evaluated through conditions, loop structures, and selections. This chapter also shows you how to do error handling in Red. We illustrate this throughout the chapter by developing a guessing-number game.

Chapter 5, *Working with Series and Blocks*, helps you to understand that blocks and series form the foundation of Red code. Developing in Red primarily means working with blocks, so that's what we will learn.

Chapter 6, *Using Functions and Objects,* deals with how to make your code more compact and readable using of functions and objects.

Chapter 7, *Working with Files*, helps you learn how to use files as a data store. We examine reading and writing files, either data files or code files. We'll develop the topic through an ongoing example of downloading currency exchange rates.

Chapter 8, *Parsing Data*, explores a first Red dialect called parse, which is specialized in analyzing data streams. We apply it to get meaningful information from the currency rates we stored previously.

Chapter 9, *Composing Visual Interfaces*, introduces a second Red dialect to build cross-platform graphical user interfaces. It builds upon Chapter 5, *Working with Series and Blocks*, and Chapter 7, *Working with Files*, to build a visual frontend for our exchange rate download, and we'll also develop a basic contacts data store app.

Chapter 10, *Advanced Red*, encounters the power of reactive programming to build highly reactive apps. You will get an idea of the foundational layer of it all, namely Red/System. Furthermore, you get to know how to interact with the operating system and use some high-performance datatypes. Also, Red's future in the blockchain programming world is discussed. Finally, we discuss what lies ahead of us, and provide some pointers to deepen the readers' Red knowledge.

To get the most out of this book

Some knowledge of the basic concepts of programming and a bit of experience of any programming language, such as Java, C#, Python, Ruby, or JavaScript, is assumed. To follow along with the examples and exercises, only a minimal install is required, which is discussed in detail in Chapter 2, *Setting Up for Development*. Practice is the best way to learn a new language. That's why each chapter contains some questions and small exercises to try out your new skills. You'll find the solution in the code files and in the Assessments section.

Download the example code files

You can download the example code files for this book from your account at www.packtpub.com. If you purchased this book elsewhere, you can visit www.packtpub.com/support and register to have the files emailed directly to you.

You can download the code files by following these steps:

1. Log in or register at `www.packtpub.com`.
2. Select the **SUPPORT** tab.
3. Click on **Code Downloads & Errata**.
4. Enter the name of the book in the **Search** box and follow the onscreen instructions.

Once the file is downloaded, please make sure that you unzip or extract the folder using the latest version of:

- WinRAR/7-Zip for Windows
- Zipeg/iZip/UnRarX for Mac
- 7-Zip/PeaZip for Linux

The code bundle for the book is also hosted on GitHub at `https://github.com/PacktPublishing/Learn-Red-Fundamentals-of-Red`. In case there's an update to the code, it will be updated on the existing GitHub repository.

We also have other code bundles from our rich catalog of books and videos available at `https://github.com/PacktPublishing/`. Check them out!

Conventions used

There are a number of text conventions used throughout this book.

`CodeInText`: Indicates code words in text, database table names, folder names, filenames, file extensions, pathnames, dummy URLs, user input, and Twitter handles. Here is an example: "The console executable is built inside the `/home/user/.red` folder and is named in the format `console-yyyy-m-dd-nnnnn`."

A block of code is set as follows:

```
Red [
    Name-Of-Info: "Value of Info"
    Name-Of-Info2: "Value of Info2"
    ...
]
```

When we wish to draw your attention to a particular part of a code block, the relevant lines or items are set in bold:

```
a: [1 2 3]
b: copy a
b ;== [1 2 3]
append a 4
a ;== [1 2 3 4]
b ;== [1 2 3]
```

You can find the code in the codefile that accompanies each section. At the start of each code snippet, you'll see:

```
;-- see ChapterNN/codefile.red:
```

This means that this snippet is found in the file `ChapterNN/codefile.red` in the code download (where NN goes from 01 to 10), as well as the code snippets shown after that, until a new codefile is indicated.

We'll use the terms program, script, app or application as synonyms in this book, because a Red source file can be compiled or interpreted.

We show the return value of a piece of code after `;==` like `a: 5   ;== 5`, because `==` is how the Red console displays it, and the prefix `;` makes it into a comment in scripts.

We have chosen to make all programs immediately runnable in the console without errors. However, certain code is there explicitly to make you see certain errors. These are indicated with a comment: `*** Script Error ....` Just remove the comment (`;`) sign at the start of the line to make the error occur.
The same goes for lines staring with `#include`, just uncomment them in order to compile the program.

Any command-line input or output is written as follows:

```
$ sudo apt-get update
```

Bold: Indicates a new term, an important word, or words that you see onscreen. For example, words in menus or dialog boxes appear in the text like this. Here is an example: "From the menu, open **File | Run**."

Warnings or important notes appear like this.

 Tips and tricks appear like this.

Get in touch

Feedback from our readers is always welcome.

General feedback: Email feedback@packtpub.com and mention the book title in the subject of your message. If you have questions about any aspect of this book, please email us at questions@packtpub.com.

Errata: Although we have taken every care to ensure the accuracy of our content, mistakes do happen. If you have found a mistake in this book, we would be grateful if you would report this to us. Please visit www.packtpub.com/submit-errata, selecting your book, clicking on the Errata Submission Form link, and entering the details.

Piracy: If you come across any illegal copies of our works in any form on the Internet, we would be grateful if you would provide us with the location address or website name. Please contact us at copyright@packtpub.com with a link to the material.

If you are interested in becoming an author: If there is a topic that you have expertise in and you are interested in either writing or contributing to a book, please visit authors.packtpub.com.

Reviews

Please leave a review. Once you have read and used this book, why not leave a review on the site that you purchased it from? Potential readers can then see and use your unbiased opinion to make purchase decisions, we at Packt can understand what you think about our products, and our authors can see your feedback on their book. Thank you!

For more information about Packt, please visit packtpub.com.

1
Red's Mission

In this chapter, we take a look at the main characteristics of Red, more specifically, what makes Red stand out compared to other programming languages. This will motivate you to start learning Red. Don't worry if some statements are a bit abstract at this stage; they will become clearer when we start using Red in the following chapters. It may be a good idea to come back to this chapter later.

We will cover the following topics:

- A short history of Red
- What makes Red special?
- Red's main features

Technical requirements

You can find the code for this chapter here: `https://github.com/PacktPublishing/Learn-Red-Fundamentals-of-Red/tree/master/Chapter01`

A short history of Red

Red is an open source, modern programming language and platform, designed and developed by *Nenad Rakocevic*. Red started out in early 2011 and is now at Version 0.6.3 (with 0.6.4 coming in the near future), aiming for a 1.0 release in the next year or so. In order to better understand its features, we have to explore its name and history a bit.

What Red stands for

Red is short for *Red[uced] REBOL*, and that's why Red users proudly call themselves *reducers*. This points to two things:

- Red builds upon REBOL, a language that gained some fame around the millennium and was built by Carl Sassenrath. In fact, Red is syntactically and semantically a 95% clone of REBOL, but tries to improve and enhance it where possible. This also means REBOL scripts can be easily converted to Red.
- Red (like REBOL) wants to reduce today's code complexity—it aims to have compact runtime environments and dependencies (around 1 MB), instead of the hundreds of MB of the Java or .NET platform.

Some history

Development of Red started out with **Red/System**—this is a low-level language (like C) to enable programming at the full system level. Red/System is like an older sibling—it looks very much like Red, but it is aimed at lower-level programming so it is more restricted. We'll come back to it in `Chapter 10`, *Advanced Red*.

Gradually, Red evolved this foundation, adding with each release more and more data types, actions, and functions. A REPL interactive coding console, execution on ARM processors, a parsing engine, a cross-platform GUI dialect (working on Windows and macOS, and nearing completion on Linux and Android), reactive programming, and macros are among the hallmarks of this evolution.

From January 2015, the **Fullstack Technologies** company was formed to continue Red's ongoing development, together with an ever-growing community of open source contributors. The company raised capital from InnovationWorks and GeekFounders (Chinese VC early-stage investors) and has its headquarters in Beijing's **Silicon Valley**.

In January 2018, Red joined the blockchain revolution—through an **Initial Coin Offering** (**ICO**) with its own cryptocurrency, RED (Red Community Token) token, and it gained a vast amount of new funding capital to sustain and accelerate its completion. Using its unique capabilities, a special dialect of Red called **Red/C3** is being built, specifically dedicated to blockchain and smart contracts programming.

Since spring 2018, the Red project has been managed by the **Red Foundation**, based in Paris (France), and also led by Nenad Rakocevic. This organization will also foster a new economic model for open source projects, using the RED token to drive development.

What makes Red special?

Here we concentrate on the characteristics that sets Red apart from other contemporary programming languages.

A full-stack language – from the metal to the meta

Together with its foundation Red/System, Red forms a *full-stack language*—this means it can be used to develop high-level applications (domain-specific languages, graphical frontends, and high-level scripting) as well as low-level programs (embedded systems, operating systems, and device drivers), as shown in the following diagram in comparison with other languages:

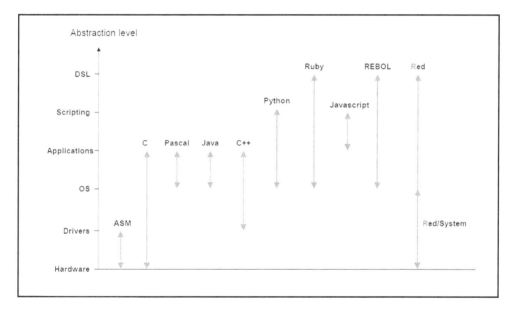

It is quite unique in programming history that a single language spans the whole programming stack. This means that you as a Red developer only have to know one language from low to high level coding!

Code is data and data is code

Red is a modern descendant of the venerable LISP programming language. Instead of LISP's cumbersome parenthesis usage, it has taken Logo's simplified syntax. Everything in LISP is some kind of *LISt Processing*, and the same goes for Red—basically all code amounts to a combination of actions on *blocks,* which is the Red equivalent to LISP lists.

A block is simply a grouping of values between rectangular brackets [ ], such as [7 13 42]. You'll soon see that blocks are the fundamental building unit in Red code. This has the consequence that only a minimal syntax is used to represent code as well as data.

It will become clear that [ ] are used a lot in Red. On English or US keyboards this is easy, with its dedicated keys for [and]. On my (Dutch) keyboard it is *ALTGR + ^* and *ALTGR + $*. On some keyboards, it is *Alt + 5* and *Alt + 6*. I find it easier to switch to US keyboard layout while coding.

Like LISP, it has a very powerful capacity—it is *homoiconic*, literally **self-representing**. What this means is that Red can work with its code just as it does with its data values, because data and code are represented the same way, namely as blocks. This makes it possible for programs to write other programs, in other words, to do *metaprogramming*. We'll see several examples of this feature in the coming chapters.

Data types built in

For you as a developer to work with data efficiently, Red has more than 45 and counting built-in data types, from common types such as integers, chars, and strings to less common ones, such as pairs, tuples, files, URLs, emails, and so on. Moreover, you use the same set of operations to work with them, which greatly eases the learning curve. To do that in other languages, you would have to create objects from specialized classes to start working with them, or even import a library. As a first example, you can add and subtract days from a date value simply as follows:

```
;-- see Chapter01/special.red:
1-Feb-2018 + 14        ; == 15-Feb-2018
1-Feb-2018 - 42        ; == 21-Dec-2017
```

Small toolchain and executables

As we will see in the next chapter, when we're setting up, the complete toolchain (compilers, standard-library, docs, and REPL) comes packaged in a minimal 1 MB file, with *no installation and configuration requirements*—here we can see the reduction at work! Compare this with a Java runtime, which is about 150x bigger, or the Python runtime which also is 50 times bigger.

After compilation, Red produces executables of sizes typically around 0.5 to 1 MB, with no dependencies needed. This simplifies deployment of apps into production enormously. This aspect, combined with the low memory footprint, makes Red a very appealing choice for mobile and embedded apps. A garbage collector, which will be integrated in one of the next releases, ensures that memory consumption stays low.

Coding in Red is very expressive and concise, reducing script size, in the range of KBs. This will become apparent in the coming chapters. Just as an example, to read a web page into a string `page` you do the following:

```
page: read http://www.red-lang.org
```

In 2013, the Redmonk website published an article (which you can view here: `http://redmonk.com/dberkholz/2013/03/25/programming-languages-ranked-by-expressiveness/`) examining the expressiveness of languages. The results were summarized in the following diagram:

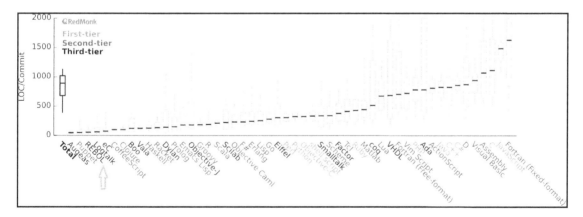

On the vertical axis, the number of lines of code per commit are depicted. We see that REBOL (Red's direct parent) scores very low compared to mainstream languages, indicating that fewer lines are needed in coding comparable tasks.

Dialects

One of Red's greatest strengths is the ability to easily create **domain-specific languages** (**DSLs**) or **dialects**. These are small and optimized sub-languages designed for a specific task, such as *parse* for transforming text (see Chapter 8, *Parsing Data*), *view* and *draw* for composing graphical user interfaces (see Chapter 9, *Composing Visual Interfaces*), and *Red/C3* for blockchain programming (see Chapter 10, *Advanced Red*).

Red's main features

As a programming language, Red embraces nearly all paradigms:

- **Imperative**: Providing everything needed for controlling code execution and error-handling (see Chapter 4, *Code Controlling Structures* and Chapter 5, *Working with Series and Blocks*)
- **Functional**: With functions as first class values (see Chapter 6, *Using Functions and Objects*)
- **Object-oriented**: Complete with inheritance, but not class-based (see Chapter 6, *Using Functions and Objects*)
- **Concurrency**: With async task support and an actor model (from v 0.9.0)
- **Symbolic**: Being able to manipulate its own code as if it was plain data (all chapters)
- **Reactive**: Included in the **GUI** (**Graphical User Interface**) system (see Chapter 9, *Composing Visual Interfaces* and Chapter 10, *Advanced Red*)

Aside from REBOL and LISP, Red has taken inspiration from the following:

- Forth and Logo for its syntax
- Lua, for its capabilities as an embedded language, and its **JIT** (**Just-In-Time**) compiler
- Self, for its prototype object-model
- Scala, for its type inference engine and compilation

Although it can be statically compiled, Red has a graphical **REPL** console (**Read Evaluate Print Loop**) like other dynamic and scripting languages, to experiment with code interactively. We will explore this console in Chapter 2, *Setting Up for Development*.

In contrast to REBOL, which is an interpreted language only, Red also *compiles to native code* through Red/System, thus achieving much better performance, something like Crystal compared to Ruby. Compared to C, at this moment Red/System is 2-4x slower.

Portability

Red runs in the Windows, Linux, Android, macOS, and FreeBSD environments in a 32-bit version (the 64-bit version is planned) with cross-compilation capability. Furthermore, it runs on ARMv5 processors and on the Raspberry Pi and Arduino boards.

Like a Swiss Army knife

The versatility of the Red platform makes it suitable for apps on the entire spectrum, such as:

- High-level scripting (for example, glue code such as Lua)
- Web apps
- GUI desktop applications
- Android apps (from Version 0.7 onward)
- 2D games
- Data processing
- Grammar parsing and constructing specialized languages
- Network/system programming, IoT devices programming, robotics

Summary

In this chapter, we looked at Red's main characteristics, and examined its place among other programming languages. In the following chapter, we will set up an environment to start up our development with Red.

Questions

1. Why does Red have a Red/System component?
2. What is a full-stack language, and why is Red an example of that?
3. What do the the Red and LISP languages have in common?
4. Give three ways in which Red reduces software complexity.
5. What is a dialect in Red? Give some examples.
6. Why is Red faster than REBOL?
7. Name some of the environments in which Red can run.

Setting Up for Development 2

Now we are going to set the stage for our future Red development. We'll get Red on to your computer, and then immediately start working in the Red console to get a feel for the environment. Then, we'll create our first script, run it in the console, and then compile and execute it. We will also discuss how Red compiles and what the different compilation options are. Finally, we'll show some coding environments to craft your Red code with ease.

We will cover the following topics:

- Installing Red
- Working interactively in the Red console
- Running and compiling your first script
- Other compilation options
- Red's compilation model
- Development environments for writing Red

Technical requirements

We'll download the Red toolchain from here: `http://www.red-lang.org/p/download.html`

You'll find the code for this chapter here: `https://github.com/PacktPublishing/Learn-Red-Fundamentals-of-Red/tree/master/Chapter02`

Installing Red

To get Red on your machine, simply download and save the latest stable version that corresponds to your **operating system** (**OS**) from here: `http://www.red-lang.org/p/download.html`. The download is named `red-num` (on Windows, the file also has an `.exe` extension), where `num` is the version number, such as 063. This small file (around 1 MB) contains the full Red toolchain, runtime library, and console source code, truly batteries included! It is that small because no external dependencies other than the OS are included.

 On the downloads page, you can also find the nightly automated build and the latest source code from the `master` branch. If you want to work with a Red version that has the latest functionalities, download the nightly master build. For regular development, you better stick with the last stable version.

Red's runtime library is written as a mix of Red and Red/System. At this time, the Red toolchain (compilers, linkers, packagers) still depends heavily on REBOL 2. For example, the current compilers for Red and Red/System are written in REBOL 2. The goal for version 1.0 or beyond is to remove this REBOL dependency, so that Red is completely self-hosted.

Installing Red on Windows

Save the file in a suitable folder (it can be installed anywhere), let's say `c:\red`. For convenience, rename the file to `red.exe`. Now double-click this file—this will then automatically build the Red GUI-console, taking a few moments.

The `gui-console-yyyy-m-dd-nnnnn.exe` file (`yyyy-m-dd` is a build date and `nnnnn` a build number) is cached on disk in the `c:\ProgramData\Red` folder. Then the Red GUI console appears, waiting for your input at the `>>` prompt:

```
Red Console                                    —    □    ×
File  Options  Help
--== Red 0.6.3 ==--                                      ^
Type HELP for starting information.

>>
                                                         ∨
```

About the version
The first line shows that the current Red version at the time of writing is 0.6.3. The stable Red 0.6.3 version has only two menu-items—File and Options. This screenshot was built from the master branch in mid-April 2018, which already shows the 0.6.4 layout. You'll probably see a higher version number in your download.

This Red console is completely written in Red.

Next time you start `red.exe`, the built-in REPL GUI console will open immediately. To make the Red toolchain available to your entire system, add the installation folder (here `c:\red`) to the `Path` environment variables using **Configuration**, **System**, **Advanced Configuration**, **Environment Variables**.

Here are some useful remarks to help you out in certain cases:

- When compiling the GUI console, some antivirus apps (such as Avast or Avira) report a Win32:Malware-gen or the like. This is because their heuristic search mechanisms signal a false positive for the binaries compiled by Red. The solution for this is to add the `C:\ProgramData\Red` folder and other folders where you compile Red executables to the **Excluded Folders** list of your antivirus software interface, so that they are whitelisted and not checked by the antivirus program.
- When Red is started in a console from a folder other than the installation folder, you can see the following error—`PROGRAM ERROR: Invalid encapsulated data`. This is a known issue (`https://github.com/red/red/issues/543`) caused by the REBOL support at this moment. Currently, running Red requires a wrapping shell script `red.bat`:
    - Rename `red.exe` to `red-exe.exe`
    - In the same folder, create a `red.bat` file with this contents:
        ```
        @"%~dp0red-exe.exe" %*
        ```
    - Now, giving the `red` command will automatically start this `red.bat` command file

Installing Red on Linux and macOS

To install Red on a Linux or macOS system, you would need to follow these steps:

1. Save the file from `http://www.red-lang.org/p/download.html` in a folder of your choice, say `/home/user/red` (where `user` is your username).

2. Rename the file `red-num` to `red`.

3. In your Terminal, go to the `red` subfolder, and do a `chmod u+x red` to give the user executable rights on the Red binary.

4. Install some 32-bit supporting libraries if you work on a 64-bit Linux system (this is needed for executing REBOL 2, which needs these libraries.) Open a Terminal app and give the following commands:

```
$ sudo dpkg --add-architecture i386
$ sudo apt-get update
$ sudo apt-get install libc6:i386 libcurl3:i386
```

5. Now simply run Red using the `red` command in a Terminal window.

The Red console will be built, but only the first time. The console executable is built inside the `/home/user/.red` folder and is named in the format `console-yyyy-m-dd-nnnnn`.

Afterwards, the command-line console opens:

To make Red available everywhere in the filesystem, add the following line to your `.profile` and `.bashrc` scripts:

export PATH=$PATH:/home/user/red

(In the preceding command, `user` is your username.)

Then, open a new Terminal app. Now the Red executable can be started from any directory.

If you have a Red Linux utility script in `/bin` like I did, you have to rename it as follows:

```
cd /bin
sudo mv red red_old
```

If you encounter an **Invalid compressed data** problem, this is the same REBOL issue as mentioned with Windows. It can be remedied by creating a shell script, `red.sh`, with the following contents:

```
#!/bin/bash
red $@
```

Don't forget to make the shell script executable with `chmod u+x red.sh`.

 An alternative to the Red command-line version in Linux is to install WineHQ (`https://www.winehq.org/`), a tool that makes it possible to run Windows programs on Linux. Then you can run the Red Windows version with the graphical console.

For Arch Linux, FreeBSD, and other specific distributions, you can find further instructions on the download page.

Red can also be installed by using the Chocolatey package manager (`https://chocolatey.org/packages/red`).

Regardless of which OS you are on, to quickly view the version number of your Red installation, open a Terminal and type:

```
red -V
```

This will give you the version *n.u.m* (for example, *0.6.3*).

A look at the source code

Red's source code can be found here: `https://github.com/red/red`. If you're curious, you can download an archive file locally (click the **Clone or download** button) and unzip it for a closer look, for example, inside your Red installation directory. Alternatively, with `git` installed on your machine, you can clone the source code with the following command:

```
git clone https://github.com/red/red.git
```

For easy reference, rename the source folder as `red-source`. Here is an overview:

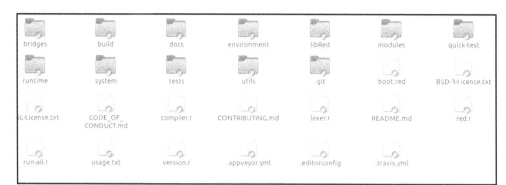

You will notice that lots of source files have a `.r` extension, which means these are REBOL files. Indeed, at this stage, the Red framework is scaffolded with REBOL. Some important files are:

- `red.r`: This is the Red and Red/System compiler
- `run-all.r`: This is the starting point for running the complete Red test suite

The goal of the Red team is to completely rewrite this scaffolding in Red and so remove the dependency on REBOL. This will probably happen in v2. Then, Red will be completely self-hosted and every new version will bootstrap from an older Red version.

At the same level as this folder, you could create a `projects` folder, in which you can start developing:

- `red`
    - `red-source`
    - `projects`
    - `red` binary or shell script

Working interactively in the Red console

Like any dynamic language, Red has a REPL console. The `red` command without arguments (open or double-click `red.bat`) starts a graphical window console on Windows and macOS, and a command-line console on Linux. If you need a command-line console on Windows and macOS, just use the command `red --cli`.

The console is a full Red interpreter and expects the input of Red code after the >> prompt, to evaluate and then execute it when pressing *Enter.* It's a live interaction with the language. Simply giving it a value (here a string indicated by "") returns that value after the ==:

```
;-- see Chapter02/console-examples.red:
>> "Red is awesome"
== "Red is awesome"
```

(You can find the source code of these examples in ch2/console-examples.red. In all code files, we'll indicate the returned output with a ;== prefix, like this, ;== "Red is awesome").

What happens if you type Red is awesome in the console? The REPL throws an error at you—Script Error: is does not allow word! for its 'field argument. Red doesn't see that the input is a string, so doesn't understand it.

Go ahead and do some calculations:

```
>> 7 * 8
== 56
>> 7*8
*** Syntax Error: invalid integer! at "7*8"
*** Where: do
*** Stack: load
>> 2.3 + 1
== 3.3
>> 7 / 4
== 1
>> 85.3 / 2.5
== 34.12
>> 8 - 10
== -2
```

In the second line, we see our first syntax error. It means that you have to use a space before and after a binary operator such as *. Notice that / using integers returns an integer result.

The console has a built-in help and documentation system that you can start by entering `?` or `help`:

```
>> ?

    Use HELP or ? to view built-in docs for functions, values
    for contexts, or all values of a given datatype:

        help append
        ? system
        ? function!

    To search for values by name, use a word:

        ? pri
        ? to-

    To also search in function specs, use a string:

        ? "pri"
        ? "issue!"

    Other useful functions:

        ??      - Display a word and the value it references
        probe  - Print a molded value
        source - Show a function's source code
        what   - Show a list of known functions or words
        about  - Display version number and build date
        quit   - Leave the Red console
```

Try out the examples to get a feel for its search and completion features (the word **molded** means: in a readable format).

Here are some other useful hints for working in the console:

- The up arrow and down arrow are used to retrieve the previous and next console commands, which can then be altered and/or re-executed. In fact, a history of the console commands is stored in the `system/console/history` block, and from version 0.6.4 this is preserved between sessions. In Chapter 6, *Working with Files*, in the *Loading and saving files* section, we'll learn a nice trick to save a history of console commands to a file for easier processing.
- To clear the screen, use *CTRL+L*.
- You can close the console at any time with the close window icon, or from the prompt by entering `q` or `quit` + *Enter* (on Linux, also with *CTRL+D*).
- *Home* and *End* position the cursor at the start and end of a line.
- Use the *Esc* key when you want to get out of a (running) statement to the prompt in the GUI console; for the command-line interface use *Ctrl+C*.

- Copy/paste code (even entire Red scripts) with the mouse or the usual keyboard shortcuts (*Ctrl+C - Ctrl+V*).
- Use `pwd` or `what-dir` to get the current folder (the folder the REPL was started in). The output will be as follows: `%/E/Red/`. `%` indicates a file path, its parts are separated by `/`.
- To change the current folder, use `cd`. For example, `cd %/E/Red/apps/google-finance`.
- Multiple Red consoles can be open at the same time.

The folder from which Red is started up is given by typing `system/options/path`.

Changing the prompt to show the time is easy and gives a glimpse of Red's power. See the following command:

```
system/console/prompt: rejoin [now/time " >> "]
;== "15:02:19 >> "
```

You can find the source code of the REPL in `red-source/environment/console`.

Running and compiling your first script

Experimenting in the REPL is fine for small code fragments and you should definitely use it, but soon you will want to keep your code in a file. Use your preferred code editor (or look at the last *Development environments for writing Red* section of this chapter for editors and IDEs with support for Red development) and type in the following text:

```
;-- see Chapter02/hello-world.red:
Red [
    Title: "Simple hello world script"
]
print "Hello Red World!"
```

Save the file as `hello-world.red`; `.red` is the extension for Red source code files.

The `Red [ ]` header block is mandatory; we'll see its purpose in the next chapter.

Executing a script in the Red console

Using the Red console, we can execute this script in five ways:

1. If it is a small script, you could just copy the code that starts after the header and paste it into the REPL.
2. Right-click on `hello-world.red` and choose **Open With**. Browse to the Red `bat` file (on Windows), and select it. The console opens up with the output message. From now on, double-clicking on a Red source file will execute it in the Red console.
3. Open a Terminal (in Windows with `cmd` or a PowerShell console; in Linux/macOS by right-clicking on a folder and choosing **Open in Terminal**) and navigate to the folder where the source file is. Then type in the command-line, `red hello-world.red`.
4. At the Red console prompt `>>`, type `do %hello-world.red` to obtain the same result. The `do` is a function that evaluates its argument, in this case a source file. This is the way to execute a script *from within* the console.

   > You will get the following **Access error** if the script file cannot be found, such as `red>> do %does-not-exist.red`:
   > `*** Access error: cannot open: %does-not-exist.red`

    To avoid this error if the file `script.red` exists, but it sits in a different folder `tests`, if `tests` is a subfolder—do `%tests/script.red`, if `tests` is a folder one level up—do `%../tests/script.red`.

   But you can also move the current active folder of the Red REPL (initially the folder where it was started) to where the file resides, by doing `cd tests` or `cd ../tests`, and then do `%script.red`

5. From the menu, open **File | Run**. A file explorer window opens where you can search for the source file. Opening it runs the code with the `do` command.

In all these cases the code is interpreted. This also means the script cannot contain Red/System code. In case you wondered, this is not **JIT** (**Just-In-Time**) compilation to native code; this is planned for a later version of Red.

If you have downloaded the Red source code as indicated in the previous section, open a Red console in that folder and run some of the demo scripts to see Red in action. For example, a universal Hello world:

```
red>> do %tests/hello.red
```

You should see the following output:

```
Hello, world!
Χαῖρε, κόσμε!
你好，世界
Dobrý den světe
```

If you take a look at the source code, you see that it just prints these strings. This shows that Unicode is no problem for Red!

Compiling a script to an executable

Now we examine two different modes for compiling a Red program.

Development mode

To compile a Red program to native code, we have to do the following:

1. Open a Terminal window and go to the folder where your script lives.
2. Give the command **red -c** `hello-world.red`.

Here is the output (on Windows in PowerShell):

```
PS E:\Red\The_book_of_Red\Chapter2-Setting-up-for-development\code> red -c hello-world.red

-=== Red Compiler 0.6.3 ===-

Compiling E:\Red\The_book_of_Red\Chapter2-Setting-up-for-development\code\hello-world.red ...
Compiling libRedRT...
...compilation time : 2407 ms

Compiling to native code...
...compilation time : 64085 ms
...linking time     : 766 ms
...output file size : 934400 bytes
...output file      : E:\Red\The_book_of_Red\Chapter2-Setting-up-for-development\code\libRedRT.dll

...compilation time : 47 ms

Target: MSDOS

Compiling to native code...
...compilation time : 1828 ms
...linking time     : 94 ms
...output file size : 67072 bytes
...output file      : E:\Red\The_book_of_Red\Chapter2-Setting-up-for-development\code\hello-world.exe
```

When a –c compilation is done, Red looks in this folder for a shared library libRedRT (.dll in Windows or .so in Linux/macOS); if this doesn't exist, it is compiled. The libRedRT shared dynamic library contains the whole compiled standard library and RunTime in precompiled form, and its size is less than 1 MB. As you can see, this compilation takes about a minute. But this only occurs the first time and is done for caching reasons. The next time, a compilation of any program in this folder is very fast:

```
PS E:\Red\The_book_of_Red\Chapter2-Setting-up-for-development\code> red -c hello-world.red

-=== Red Compiler 0.6.3 ===-

Compiling E:\Red\The_book_of_Red\Chapter2-Setting-up-for-development\code\hello-world.red ...
...using libRedRT built on 7-Feb-2018/10:08:52+1:00
...compilation time : 31 ms

Target: MSDOS

Compiling to native code...
...compilation time : 1531 ms
...linking time     : 78 ms
...output file size : 67072 bytes
...output file      : E:\Red\The_book_of_Red\Chapter2-Setting-up-for-development\code\hello-world.exe

PS E:\Red\The_book_of_Red\Chapter2-Setting-up-for-development\code>
```

This is compiling in Development mode, which is the default. When working on the same code, subsequent compilations are much faster. The result in this case is a native binary `hello-world.exe`; so run it as `./hello-world.exe` to show the hello message. It needs the `libRedRT` library in the same folder to run!

```
PS E:\Red\The_book_of_Red\Chapter2-Setting-up-for-development\code> ./hello-world.exe
Hello Red World!
```

 The code in `libRedRT` won't change unless you update your Red version. Upgrading the Red binary to a newer version will automatically upgrade `libRedRT` on first invocation. If needed, you can run a `red clear` command in your compilation folder to remove all files from a previous version. If your script contains Red/System code, use `red -u` or `red --update-libRedRT` to rebuild `libRedRT` and compile the script.

Release mode

When development and testing are finished, and you are ready to deploy to production, you'll want to compile your code to one standalone executable that includes `libRedRT` and all other needed dependencies. This is done with the **red -r** `hello-world.red` command, forcing release mode with the `-r` flag. Here you see screen output from a compilation on Windows:

```
PS E:\Red\The_book_of_Red\code\ch2> red -r hello-world.red

-=== Red Compiler 0.6.3 ===-

Compiling E:\Red\The_book_of_Red\code\ch2\hello-world.red ...
...compilation time : 1418 ms

Target: MSDOS

Compiling to native code...
...compilation time : 40118 ms
...linking time     : 300 ms
...output file size : 596480 bytes
...output file      : E:\Red\The_book_of_Red\code\ch2\hello-world.exe

PS E:\Red\The_book_of_Red\code\ch2>
```

The compilation time is a lot longer in this mode, but you'll need to do it only once. The resulting binary size is somewhat increased (it contains the runtime and makes additional runtime functions available), but still quite small. To deploy, you only have to copy the resulting binary to your production environment.

 This compile mode is also required when the program contains `#include` statements, or when it contains Red/System code.

The Red consoles can be found in the source code `/environment/console` folder, respectively in the CLI and GUI subfolders. The consoles are included in the Red toolchain, but with what we now know, we can compile and then use them separately like this:

```
red -r console.red
```

Here is the command to compile the GUI console:

```
red -r -t Windows gui-console.red
```

 To include any graphical stuff, you have to add the `-t` platform flag, as `-t Windows` in the preceding command.

Other compilation options

To see the documentation on the `red` command, type `red -h` in a Terminal. Here are some useful options:

- Use `-o` to name the output binary differently.
- Use `-d` in debugging mode. Functions used to print debug info (such as `print` and `probe`) show their output in the Red console.
- Use `-dlib` to make a shared library from code, for example, for a code file containing only functions.
- Use `-e` in combination with either `-c` or `-r` to compile in encapped mode; the runtime will be compiled and included in a single binary, together with your script. However, your script is not compiled; it is converted to a special format (Redbin) and compressed. The result is a standalone executable, and your script will be run by the interpreter. This can be useful when you encounter a compiler limitation, but your code can still be interpreted.

One of the amazing features of the Red compiler is its cross-compilation capability, to build an executable for a platform other than the one your are developing on. That is done with the –t flag as follows:

```
red -t TargetID hello-world.red
```

Here, *TargetID* can take the following values:

- MSDOS: Windows, x86, console (+ GUI) applications
- Windows: Windows, x86, GUI applications
- WindowsXP: Windows, x86, GUI applications, no touch API
- Linux: GNU/Linux, x86
- Linux-ARM: GNU/Linux, ARMv5, armel (soft-float)
- RPi: GNU/Linux, ARMv5, armhf (hard-float)
- Darwin: macOS Intel, console-only applications
- macOS: macOS Intel, applications bundles
- Syllable: Syllable OS, x86
- FreeBSD: FreeBSD, x86
- Android: Android, ARMv5
- Android-x86: Android, x86

So, if I wanted to generate a Linux executable that is named `hello-linux`, I would do the following:

```
red -t Linux -o hello-linux hello-world.red
```

For each of the `-flag` options, there exists a corresponding `--option`. For example, `--release` is the same as `-r`, and `--target` the same as `-t`. The verbose version makes command-line scripts more readable. Type `red -h` in a Terminal to see the full list.

Red's compilation model

From the previous screenshot of a `red -r` release-mode compilation, we see that this takes two steps:

1. The first step doesn't state it explicitly, but it compiles the Red source code to Red/System code.

2. The second one compiles Red/System to native code:

As mentioned, compilation is done with the REBOL `red.r` script. Due to this, Red is currently 32-bit only, self-hosting will make 64-bit binaries possible.

If you are feeling adventurous, you can experiment with compiling Red from within the REBOL console. Visit: `https://github.com/red/red#running-red-from-the-sources-for-contributors`

At this moment, there are two distinct modes of executing a Red program:

- Running with the interpreter, which takes place in memory and involves some amount of compilation
- Compiling to native code in a binary file and then running this executable, with Red/System as an intermediate step

The definitive compiler architecture will be more complicated than in other languages and could be called a **collaborative execution model**; the compiler will work in collaboration with a JIT compiler and an interpreter.

Development environments for writing Red

You basically need no more than a simple text editor and a Terminal for compiling work. However, some syntax highlighting and perhaps a built-in compile and run system can make your life much easier.

Simple text editors

Notepad++ is a free and versatile source code editor that only runs on Windows. In the article at `http://helpin.red/Setup-Notepad.html`, you can see how to build it out to a Red dev environment. Everedit (`http://www.everedit.net/`), Crimson Editor (`http://www.crimsoneditor.com/`), and emacs (`https://www.gnu.org/software/emacs/`) also provide syntax highlighting modes.

A handy little Windows editor is Ride (`http://www.mikeparr.info/redlang.html`), written in Delphi by Mike Parr:

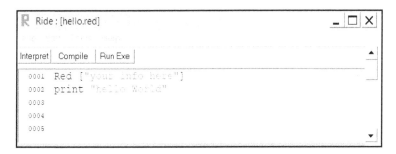

To make it work with Red's latest version, use **Tools** | **Configure Red System** from the menu to navigate to your Red binary or shell script.

More sophisticated editors

Sublime Text (`https://www.sublimetext.com/`) offers a cross-platform solution. It may be downloaded and evaluated for free; however, a license must be bought for continued use. Some Red plugins are available, such as Sublime-Red (`https://github.com/Oldes/Sublime-Red`) or Rebol-Red-Sublime (`https://github.com/onetom/rebol-red-sublime`). They offer nice syntax highlighting, code snippets, and an easy way to integrate a build system.

By far the best and most complete cross-platform option at this time is `Visual Studio Code` with the plugin (`https://marketplace.visualstudio.com/items?itemName=red-auto.red`) developed by the Red team. It has many functions, such as auto-completion, code snippets, and built-in documentation for functions when hovering over the function word, as well as syntax highlighting and typical text editor functionality.

There is a Red shortcut menu, which is *Ctrl+K, Ctrl+M. F6* interprets and *F7* compiles the current Red file with a completely integrated Terminal (PowerShell console in Windows). Here is a typical screenshot:

Actually, Red would lend itself quite well to building a dedicated **IDE** (**Interactive Development Environment**). This is a tremendous amount of work and certainly no priority for the Red core team, but perhaps some day it may appear as a community effort.

Meanwhile, here are some editors written in Red; they are not meant to be complete, but they show what you can do with very little Red code—RedEd (http://www.mycode4fun.co.uk/text-editors), AutoRed (http://www.mycode4fun.co.uk/red-apps), and Tired (http://www.mikeparr.info/tired.html) (35 lines of code!).

Summary

By now, you should have a running development environment and be able to work with the Red console. You have also learned how to compile and execute a simple script, in development mode as well as in release mode. You learned the most important compilation options, such as renaming the output file with −o, or cross-compiling your program to another deployment platform with −t. You also gained some insight into Red's compilation model. Finally, we reviewed the existing editor options and prepared a comfortable environment to start coding, working interactively with the Red console as well as with source files.

In the following chapter, we'll explore the basic building blocks of a Red program—words, values, and their types.

Questions

1. Use `print` to print out `Hello Red world!` then use `prin`. What's the difference? Look it up with `?` Now use `prn`. What happens and why?
2. What is the purpose of the `red.r` script?
3. What is a self-hosting language?
4. Which function must you use to execute a script from within the console?
5. Do you need `libRedRT` in release mode?
6. If not, then where is its code?
7. Which Red development environment gives you code completion?

Using Words, Values, and
Types

3

In this chapter, we look at the basic building blocks of a Red program—*words* and *values*. We discuss the different *types* available in Red, and what you can do with them. Some of the explanations may sound a bit dry at this moment, but because Red is quite different from other languages, you need to get a good understanding of its philosophy. Do try out the examples in the Red console! Things will also become more clear when we dive into code.

We will cover the following topics:

- Understanding words and values
- Some common datatypes
- Using blocks and parens
- Word bindings
- More about types
- Evaluating expressions and blocks
- The structure of a Red program

Technical requirements

You'll find the code for this chapter here (`https://github.com/PacktPublishing/Learn-Red-Fundamentals-of-Red/tree/master/Chapter03`). If you installed Red as indicated in `Chapter 2`, *Setting Up for Development*, you are good to go. You can work on Windows, macOS, or Linux. Certainly for this chapter, you can type or paste any code in the Red console to see its results.

Understanding words and values

A text in any language consists of *words* that have meaning, such as *total*, *temperature*, and *values*, which carry a data value, for example, 500 and 37.5°C. A program or script written in the Red language, likewise, consists of a series of words, which represent *code*, and values, which represent *data*. When executing a program, Red has to *evaluate* every word to obtain a value. Every value in Red source code has a *type*.

A word can, for example, be a name for a variable or a function, either created by the developer or built into the language. All the different words in a program, whether predefined or user-created, form its *dictionary*. By using well-chosen words for variables, blocks, objects, and functions, you can mold your Red code into almost any specific language for your application.

Type the command `what` in the console to get an overview of the *predefined words* (for the code in this section, see `Chapter03/words-and-values.red`):

```
>> what
    %          op!       Returns what is left over when one value is divided by another.
    *          op!       Returns the product of two values.
    **         op!       Returns a number raised to a given power (exponent).
    +          op!       Returns the sum of the two values.
    -          op!       Returns the difference between two values.
    /          op!       Returns the quotient of two values.
    //         op!       {Wrapper for MOD that handles errors like REMAINDER. Negligible values
    <          op!       Returns TRUE if the first value is less than the second.
    <<         op!       [data [integer!] bits [integer!]]
    <=         op!       Returns TRUE if the first value is less than or equal to the second.
    <>         op!       Returns TRUE if two values are not equal.
    =          op!       Returns TRUE if two values are equal.
    ==         op!       Returns TRUE if two values are equal, and also the same datatype.
    =?         op!       Returns TRUE if two values have the same identity.
    >          op!       Returns TRUE if the first value is greater than the second.
    >=         op!       Returns TRUE if the first value is greater than or equal to the second.
    >>         op!       [data [integer!] bits [integer!]]
    >>>        op!       [data [integer!] bits [integer!]]
    ?          function! Displays information about functions, values, objects, and datatypes.
    ??         function! Prints a word and the value it refers to (molded).
    a-an       function! Returns the appropriate variant of a or an (simple, vs 100% grammatical
    about      function! Print Red version information.
```

We can see that there are operators (type `op!`), such as * and <, and functions (type `function!`), such as `cos` and `to-integer`. Scrolling down, you can see `action!` words, such as `append` and `delete`. The same actions can apply to very different datatypes, as we will see shortly. This is called *polymorphism*; it greatly reduces the number of words that are needed in the language. Some words are `native!` such as `if` or `list-env`, or `routine!` such as `ask`, which means that they are coded in Red/System.

Unlike other programming languages, Red has *no keywords*. There are no restrictions on what words are used or how they are used—as in every language the meaning is provided by the *context* in which the words are used. For example, Red has a `print` function for printing values, but you can define your own function called `print` and use it instead of the predefined function (in fact, we do that in the *Code is data and data is code* section in `Chapter 6`, *Using Functions and Objects*). Unnecessary syntax is also kept to a minimum in Red, improving readability and simplifying code parsing.

Red uses human-friendly and recognizable formats for values to make scripts more readable, for example, `2017-10-31` or `11%`; no special constructor is needed. In some cases, more than one format for a certain type of value is accepted to allow for international variations, such as `31/Oct/2017`. Every value has a *datatype* that derives from its format, such as `date!` or `percent!` in the previous examples. Every datatype name ends in a `!` by convention. We'll encounter the most common datatypes in the following section.

During the evaluation of a program, Red classifies the value of every word as a specific datatype and acts accordingly.

Everything in Red has a datatype, even datatypes have the type `datatype!`

Words are evaluated in sequence, and they must have a value. If there is an unknown word, such as `xyz`, you get this error message—`Script Error: xyz has no value`. This is probably the most common error you will encounter at the start of your Red journey. The simplest way to give a word a value is done by adding a colon after the word, followed by the data we want to associate it with, for example:

```
room-number: 42
```

⇒ Now answer question 1 from the *Questions* section.

Words are used for naming variables, functions, actions, and objects. They are separated from each other by spaces, a line break, or one of these characters—`[ ] ( ) { } " : ; /` . So a space, a line break, or one of these characters also means the end of the (preceding) word.

Words are formed from a non-numeric character followed by alphabetic characters, so append is a word, but 7lucky is not a valid word. Like in human languages, words are not case sensitive (so City, city, and CITY are the same word) and can include hyphens (-) and a few other special characters such as + - ` * ! ~ & ? |. Multiple parts in a name are preferably separated by a dash or hyphen, such as -.

Here are some valid words:

```
is-integer?
date-of-birth
date!
*new-line*
Area51
```

Some characters such as @ # $ % ^ and , are not allowed in words—they are used to indicate specific datatypes, such as % for a percent! value.

⇒ Now answer question 2 from the *Questions* section.

As you can see, system is a special object used to hold many values required by the runtime library. You can access each of its parts with a path separator / like this—system/build or system/platform.

?? system/options reveals some internal information, as follows:

```
>> ?? system/options
system/options:
make object! [
    boot: %/E/Red/red-exe.exe
    home: none
    path: %/E/Red/
    script: none
    cache: %/C/Users/CVO/AppData/Roaming/Red/
    thru-cache: none
    args: none
```

Some common datatypes

Red has many predefined datatypes. A developer can work just as easily with often-used data such as files, images, emails, and URLs, by using the same actions and functions. You can see a list of the available types in the console by typing ? datatype!. Here are some examples (see Chapter03/common-datatypes.red):

- integer! such as -42.

- `float!` such as `1.23` or `1.23e12`; the European format `1,23` is also recognized; integers are signed 32 bits (4 bytes), floats are 64 bit.
- `logic!` such as `true` or `false`, but also `on` or `off` and `yes` or `no`, better known as Boolean values.
- `char!` such as `#"a"`, which are Unicode code points in the integer range hexadecimal `00` to `10FFFF`.
- `string!` such as `"Red is awesome"`. To work with multiline strings or strings that contain `""`, enclose them within `{ }`, such as `{She said "Hi"}`.
- `time!` such as `20:05:32`
- `date!` such as `20-Apr-2018`, `2018-04-18`, in international format such as `20-4-2018`, or with a time such as `2018-4-20/12:32`, the current date is given by `now`, and the current time by `now/time`.
- `tuple!` such as `0.6.4` or `199.4.80.7` are useful for version numbers, RGB color values, and network addresses.
- `file!` such as `%"C:\Users\Peter\Documents\cv.txt"`, `%/c/windows/`, `%/home/users/Peter/Documents/cv.txt`, or `%../scripts/*.red`.
- `tag!` such as `<font color="blue">` and useful for working with markup languages such as HTML and XML.
- `email!` such as `pres@oval.whitehouse.gov`.
- `url!` such as `http://www.red-lang.org/` or other forms starting with a scheme name such as `ftp:` or `mailto:`.
- `pair!` such as `100x50` used to indicate positions, points, or sizes.
- `issue!` such as `#MFG-932-741-A` or `#0000-1234-5678-9999` and useful for identification numbers, such as telephone numbers, model numbers, or credit card numbers.
- `binary!` are byte series of any length, encoded directly as hexadecimal (base 16), such as `#{526564206973206265617546966756C}`, base-2, such as `2#{010001}`, or base-64, such as `64#{ffff}` (which is the number `8255455`). They are used to store raw data such as images, audio, and movie files, and when encrypting data.

In every case, there is something in the syntax to distinguish it from other values so the compiler can automatically recognize their type. Each datatype has a range of possible values, a number of operations that can be performed on its values, and a different storage in memory. For every datatype there exists a corresponding function ending with a ? to test whether or not a value is of that type, for example:

```
integer? -42        ;== true
```

```
logic? off            ;== true
date? 20-4-2018       ;== true
date? 2018-44-18      ;*** Script Error: cannot MAKE/TO date! from: [day
month year]
```

Using blocks and parens

Words and any type of values can be combined in *blocks* delimited by square brackets [ ]. A block is of type block!. Here is a block containing *data*:

```
;-- Chapter03/blocks.red:
[
    "Jeff" Jeff@amz.com #213-555-1010
    "Bill" billg@ms.com #315-555-1234
    "Steve" jobs@apl.com #408-555-4321
]
```

(In the graphical REPL on Windows and macOS, this can be copied and pasted in this layout. On Linux, where there is only a console REPL at the moment, it is not so nicely formatted).

You can convert any argument to a block with to-block—to-block {1 2 3} ;== [1 2 3].

Blocks can also contain *code instructions*, like this:

```
loop 10 [prin "hello" print " world"]
```

In the following code snippet, the first block [site action] contains words, which must have a value, while the second block contains code:

```
foreach [site action] sites [
    data: read site
    do action
]
```

As you can see, there is hardly any difference between code and data; this will become clearer in the following chapters. A block doesn't evaluate itself, it only does this when called with do (see the *Evaluation with do and reduce* section) or in a code context.

In most cases, the *order* of values or words in a block is important—a block is an example of a *series*.

Of course, blocks can contain other blocks, for example: `[ [125 12] [256 26] ]`

The minimal Red script is, `Red []`, or as follows:

```
Red [
]
```

It does nothing, but it contains a required header block, which as we will see later can contain information about the script. In fact, every script file itself is also a block—it does not include the brackets, but a block that contains the whole source code is implied.

Another datatype we haven't mentioned yet is `paren!`. In the same way a `block!` is any series within brackets `[]`, a `paren!` is any series within parentheses `()`, for example, `(1 + 2)`. In contrast to blocks, a paren always evaluates itself—`(1 + 2) ;== 3`.

Red has a function called `quote`, which is special in that it does NOT evaluate its argument. Using it, we can show the `paren!` type, by asking for `type?` (we will discuss this further in the *Word bindings* section):

```
quote (1 + 2)        ;== (1 + 2)
type? quote (1 + 2)  ;== paren!
```

Comments

Interspersed throughout a program you can find comments, which is text to explain code to humans and ignored by Red. A comment starts after a semicolon (`;`) at the start or in the middle of a line:

```
;-- see Chapter03/comments.red:
; single-line comment
print "start" ; comment on a code line
```

A multiline comment is formed as follows:

```
comment {
    This is a multiline comment.
    This explains how this program works.
}
```

From the next section on, we will show the return value of a word on the same line in a comment starting with `;==` like this—`;== value`. However, `==` is also the way the REPL shows the return value, so this should be familiar.

Make multiline comments using several single-line comments (Visual Studio Code has a menu-item for this—**Edit / Toggle Line Comment**) and even use `;` `--` for a stronger visual clue. Where possible, avoid comments by choosing descriptive names, and use documentation strings (we'll cover these in `Chapter 6`, *Using Functions and Objects*) instead of comments.

Word bindings

Within a Red program, several *contexts* can exist. A context is a scope in which a word can be defined, or as reducers say—*a word is bound to a context*. For example, within a function context a local word `price` may be used, and in another function the same word `price` may have a totally different meaning or value—the word `price` is used in different contexts.

Other types of contexts are within a block or within the entire script or environment (the *global context*). For example, if you put in `type ? chocolate` in the Red console, it prints the following:

```
No matching values were found in the global context.
```

Within a context, a *word refers to a value,* as in these examples:

```
;-- see Chapter03/bindings.red:
age: 62
is-integer?: false
lunch-time: 12:32
birth-day: 17-Jan-1997
friends: ["Jeff" "Paula" "Viviane"]
```

The preceding words are bound to the global context, and refer to the values mentioned. For example, the `age` word here exists in the global context and refers to the integer value `62`, the same goes for the word `friends`, which refers to the block value `["Jeff" "Paula" "Viviane"]`.

The general syntax for *a word* `var` *referring to a value* `val` is:

```
var: val
```

No terminator (such as a semicolon) is required at the end, but there has to be a space between the : and the value.

 It is important to note that the : is not an assignment operator such as in most other programming languages. It only binds the word before it to the result of the expression following the :. In Red, `var:` has its own type called `set-word!`

`var` simply returns the value, `:var`, which is called *getting the value of the word* `var`, has the same effect, as is shown with the variable `age`:

```
age      ; == 62   <-- remember: this comment shows the value of age
:age     ; == 62
```

As with `var:`, `:var` has its own type called `get-word!`.

If it doesn't harm readability, you can place bindings on one line:

```
n: 12    m: 42
```

Multiple variables can be set to a single value in one line, like this:

```
age: number: size: 62
```

You can also use set combined with a block to give a number of words the same value:

```
set [log-time start-time run-time] 10:57  ; == 10:57:00
start-time                                ; == 10:57:00
log-time                                  ; == 10:57:00
run-time                                  ; == 10:57:00
```

`age`, `is-integer?`, `lunch-time`, `birth-day`, and `friends` are all *words*. Words are the nearest thing Red has to variables from other programming languages; that's why we will sometimes speak of variables. But keep in mind—they are *words that refer to values.*

To check if a word has a value, use the `value?` function:

```
value? age   ; == true
```

⇒ Now answer question 3 from the *Questions* section.

Use `print var` or `prin var` to output the formatted value of a variable `var` (with or without a newline) in a script. Use `probe var` to view the raw data in its type notation, which is useful for debugging, as are `?` and `??`:

```
print friends ;== Jeff Paula Viviane
probe friends ;== ["Jeff" "Paula" "Viviane"]
? friends    ;== FRIENDS is a block! value. length: 3 ["Jeff" "Paula"
"Viviane"]
?? friends   ;== friends: ["Jeff" "Paula" "Viviane"]
```

⇒ Now answer question 4 from the *Questions* section.

It is useful to mention here two other related functions:

- `form` returns a user-friendly string representation of a value, such as the following:

```
form friends        ;== "Jeff Paula Viviane"
```

  As you can see, it generates *regular text* from a block, so it's mostly used in string and text manipulation.

- `mold` returns a source format multiline string representation of a value:

```
mold friends        ;== {["Jeff" "Paula" "Viviane"]}
```

Its basic usage is to produce Red text that can be saved and re-loaded to recreate the original values.

When an output involves many parts, `print` is often used with a block, as follows:

```
name: "John"
print ["My name is:" name]     ;== My name is: John
```

The parts are automatically spaced. Special names exist for certain characters, such as `tab`, `newline` (also as character `#"^/"`), `lf` (`linefeed`), and more.

If you want to know the type of a variable, use `type?`:

```
type? age          ;== integer!
type? birth-day    ;== date!
type? friends      ;== block!
```

Inferring types

Everything in Red has a type, but as you noticed you don't have to declare that type yourself, in contrast to languages such as Java, C#, or C++. We could say that Red is a dynamic, high-level scripting language such as Python or Ruby, and so doesn't need explicit typing. This is partly true, but nevertheless Red can be compiled to native code, so the compiler needs to know the types of all words.

As many other languages do, the Red compiler *infers* the types. This *type inference* can become very complicated, leading to slow compilation. To remedy this, Red has chosen for a *hybrid type-system* (as did Crystal, Dart, and Scala), also called *optional* or *gradual typing*. This means that types can be omitted. But when they are used, the compiler can do its job much quicker, generating faster code and detect more programming errors. We'll see in Chapter 6, *Using Functions and Objects*, that types can be used in functions for function arguments and return values.

Assigning and copying

When you assign a variable to another variable, that new variable points to the same value as the first variable:

```
;-- see Chapter03/bindings.red:
a: [1 2 3]
b: a
b ;== [1 2 3]
```

Here, b returns the value in the console, inside a script you would use probe b or print b. We could show this visually as follows:

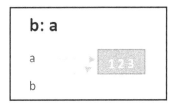

If the value of a changes, for example, by appending 4, we see that b still has the same value as a, which is evident because it points to the same value storage in memory:

```
append a 4
a ;== [1 2 3 4]
b ;== [1 2 3 4]
```

Here's a visual representation that can help you grasp it better:

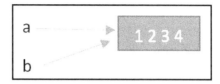

It works like that for more complex objects that are allocated on the heap with a pointer, such as the block in the example. For simple types that are allocated in the stack, such as numbers and dates, each variable gets its own value storage so that you get this behavior:

```
a: 20 ;== 20
b: a  ;== 20
a: 25 ;== 25
b     ;== 20
```

If you don't want this behavior, you have to do b: copy a, instead of b: a as shown here:

```
a: [1 2 3]
b: copy a
b ;== [1 2 3]
append a 4
a ;== [1 2 3 4]
b ;== [1 2 3]
```

Here's another visual representation to help you:

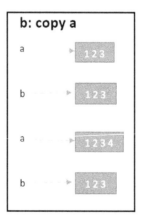

With `copy`, the value is effectively copied; b doesn't refer to the same value storage as a. And if a changes its value through *a new binding*, b retains its old value:

```
a: [1 2 3 4 5]
b   ;== [1 2 3]
```

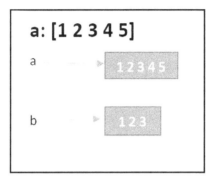

`copy` is used a lot in Red code. Basically, it is used at every initialization of a variable (except for integers, dates, and chars). If you want truly independent copies, use `copy`! For example, `daily-sales-list: copy []`.

Working with words

In this section, we dive deeper into how Red uses words.

This section goes into the very essence of Red, but its depth and subtlety can overwhelm you. Don't worry if this happens. It is not essential knowledge at this time, and you can safely come back to it later.

Prefixing a word with an apostrophe ('), such as `'b`, treats the word *literally. The value of* `'b` *is the word* b *itself,* b *is not evaluated and is treated as a symbol;* the type of `'b` is `lit-word!`:

```
;-- see Chapter03/bindings.red:
b: [1 2 3]
'b ;== b
type? 'b ;== word!
```

Why then does `type?` `'b` give `word!` as a return value? This is because `type?` is a function (as are `get` and `set`, which we'll cover next), a function evaluates its argument(s), and the evaluation of `'b` results in a `word!`. So we can also say the following:

```
c: 'b          ; == b
type? c        ; == word!
```

We can prove that the type of `'b` is `lit-word!` by using the `quote` function (see the *Using blocks and parens* section), which, as an exception among functions, does not evaluate its argument. So we have the following:

```
type? b          ; == block!
type? 'b         ; == word!
type? quote 'b   ; == lit-word!
```

`get` returns the value a *word* refers to—**get** `'b` ; == `[1 2 3]`.

`:b` (see the *Word bindings* section) has the same effect as `get` `'b`—it retrieves the value of the word `b` from Red's dictionary. Likewise, you can change a value with `set`:

```
set 'b [0 1 2]       ; == [0 1 2]
b                    ; == [0 1 2]
```

`set 'b [0 1 2]` has the same effect as `b: [0 1 2]`.

Back in the *Word bindings* section we saw that we can test with `value?` if a word exists in the dictionary. If word `a` does not refer to a value yet, `value?` `a` returns the `Script Error: a has no value`. To get `value?` to return `false`, we must use it with `'a` as an argument:

```
value? a    ;*** Script Error: a has no value
value? 'a   ;== false
```

A word that doesn't refer to any value is of type `unset!`:

```
type? get/any 'a ; == unset!
```

(Here, we have to use `get` with its refinement `/any` to avoid getting an error.)

You can remove a word from memory with `unset`—after `unset` `'b`, b no longer has a value.

More about types

Sometimes, converting a data value from one type to another is needed in programming, so here we see how to do that in Red. We also get more insight into how all Red types are connected together.

Converting types

A type determines the operations you can perform on its values; for example, adding strings doesn't exist in Red:

```
;-- see Chapter03/converting-types.red:
"12" + "34"
*** Script Error: + does not allow string! for its value1 argument
*** Where: +
```

If what we really meant was adding two integers, then we must first convert the strings to integers with to-integer:

```
(to-integer "12") + (to-integer "34")   ; == 46
```

What happens if you remove the first pair of parentheses? Could you explain this?

 When we remove the first pair of parentheses like in to-integer "12" + (to-integer "34"), we get the *** Script Error: + does not allow string! for its value1 argument. This is because + cannot add the string "12" to the integer 34.

Here are some other examples:

```
pi-str: to-string pi        ;== "3.141592653589793"
f1: to-float 42             ;== 42.0
```

You see that all these functions (each type has a conversion function) have the form to-type. You can look them all up by typing ? to- in the console.

Of course, not all conversions can succeed, such as converting an alphanumerical string to an integer, which yields a script error:

```
to-integer "34A" ;*** Script Error: cannot MAKE/TO integer! from: "34A"
```

Some of these conversion functions are very flexible. Here is an example of turning a block of three integers into a time value:

```
to-time [12 03 22] ;== 12:03:22
```

Anything can be turned into a string with `to-string`. Instead of `to-string`, often `form` or `mold` are used. Converting a string to other values (here to an integer) can also be done with `load`:

```
n: mold 3      ;== "3"
m: load "45"   ;== 45
type? m        ;== integer!
```

An alternative notation is to use the `to` action with the datatype (ending with `!`) as an argument:

```
to string! pi           ;== "3.141592653589793"
pi-int: to integer! pi  ;== 3
to float! 42            ;== 42.0
```

⇒ Now answer question 5 from the *Questions* section.

The type system

To get some idea of how Red's types are linked together, here is a schema with Red's types (you can refer to it whenever you encounter a new type; the ones we encounter in this book are printed in bold):

```
                              any-type!
          internal!
                               default!
                                        external!
                 bitset!                             event!
unset!
         map!
              any-function!                      any-object!
 native! action! op! function! routine!        object!    error!


              immediate!                        series!


datatype!    none!  logic!  refinement!  issue!
    handle!
       typeset!    scalar!            binary!    vector!            any-block!
                                      image!


 char! number! time! date! pair! tuple!  any-word!        any-list!         any-path!
                          word! lit-word!    set-word!
  integer! any-float!
       float! percent!      get-word!              block! hash! paren!


                              any-string!          path! lit-path!
                                                                    set-path!
                 string!
            file!    url!         tag!  email!          get-path!
```

You see that types are defined in a hierarchy, and the root type is any-type!. Red also defines sets of datatypes, such as scalar!, any-string!, or any-block!.

Furthermore, integer!, float!, and percent! are all number! types. Types such as scalar! or number! are called typeset! values, they are sets of types. However, any-type! is the typeset! value that contains all other types.

none! is the type of the none value, which is like null or nil in other languages, meaning that there is no value. For example, when you try to get the fifth item from a series with three items, the result is none:

```
pick [1 2 3] 5   ;== none
```

From the diagram, you can see that blocks, as well as strings, are series. The `series!` typeset is used to manage lists of all kinds of types—strings, files, email accounts, data in network ports, values returned from database systems, graphic screen layouts, and so on. Red consistently applies the same concepts and methods to interact with them, as we shall see in `Chapter 5`, *Working with Series and Blocks*, and beyond. So you only have to learn a single set of skills to be proficient in Red!

Evaluating expressions and blocks

Before getting into real programming, we need to see how we can work with Boolean values and numbers. Red is different from other programming languages, in that it does not impose the usual mathematical evaluation order, so we will take some time to investigate that. Furthermore, we will learn how `do` and `reduce` are used to evaluate.

Some basic operations

What can we do with logical values and strings, and how do we compare values and variables? Let's look at this in the following sections.

Working with Boolean values

You can work with Boolean values using the usual `and`, `or`, `xor`, and `not` operations.

Often you need to use parentheses around the conditions to make it clear for the compiler, for example, `if (4 < 5) and (6 < 7) [print "ok"] ;== ok`.

However, `complement` is like `not` for Boolean, but it gives a bitwise opposite value for other types.

⇒ Now answer question 6 from the *Questions* section.

How do you compare two values? For example, `n: 13` and `m: 42`:

- Use = (or `equal?` as an infix operator) to see if the values are the same (just like in mathematics!):

```
;-- see Chapter03/evaluation.red:
n = m              ;== false
13 = 13.0          ;== true
equal? 13 13.0     ;== true
"red" = "Red"      ;== true
```

- Use <> (or `not-equal?`) to see if the values are different:

```
n <> m         ;== true
```

- Use == (or `strict-equal?`) to see if the values are the same *and* have the same datatype. For strings, they must also have the same case, as shown in the last example:

```
13 == 13           ;== true
13 == 13.0         ;== false
"red" == "Red"     ;== false
```

- Use =? (or `same?`) to see if the values have the same identity, that is, they point to the same memory location:

```
13 =? 13       ;== true
a: 14          ;== 14
b: a           ;== 14
a = b          ;== true
a == b         ;== true
a =? b         ;== true
```

Besides these, there are the usual <, <=, >, and >= operators and corresponding functions.

⇒ Now answer questions 7-9 from the *Questions* section.

Here are two words you'll see very commonly used in Red to evaluate a block with `logic!` values:

- `all`, which is only `true` when all values in a block are `true`, for example, using n and m as previously:

```
all [n = 13   m = 42]  ;== true
all [n = 12   m = 42]  ;== none
```

- `any`, which is `true` when at least one value in a block is true, for example, **any** `[n = 12 m = 42] ;== true`

Evaluation of the values in the block proceeds from left to right, and stops at the first `false` (for `all`) or the first `true` (for `any`).

Working with numbers

The operations on numbers (`+`, `-`, `*`, `/`) can take two forms:

- The *infix* notation: n `*` m
- A more *functional* word notation, first the function, then the arguments: `multiply n m`

You can calculate the remainder of a division with `%` or `//` (`remainder` or `modulo`). Common logarithmic and trigonometric functions are available, together with functions to calculate the maximum and minimum of two numbers (`max` and `min`). Logical functions such as `even?`, `positive?`, or `zero?` test common conditions in calculations, and a versatile `round` function is available:

```
round 2.35          ;== 2.0
round 2.5           ;== 3.0
round/to pi 0.001 ;== 3.142 ; rounds to 0.001
```

Here we see a first example, `/to`, of a so-called *refinement*. It is a kind of flag that is appended to the action or function to modify its behavior. You can look them up in the console with the `?` command.

Integers can also be represented as a hexadecimal number with h as a suffix. For example, `32` and `20h` are the same number. Convert a decimal integer to hexadecimal with `to-hex`, for example:

```
to-hex 32               ;== #00000020
to-integer #00000020  ;== 32
```

If a number is too big for the 32-bit integer range, it is automatically converted to `float!`.

⇒ Now answer question 10 from the *Questions* section.

Making random objects

The `random` function can work on any value of a simple type to return a random value of that type, for example:

```
random 100         ;== 71
random 2.71        ;== 2.027808184808962
random "house"     ;== "hsuoe"
random 2018-02-13 ;== 23-Mar-1968
```

This command also has a few refinements:

- To pick a random value from a series, use `/only`:

```
random/only ["one" "two" "three" "four"]   ;== "three"
```

- `/seed` restarts the random generator to obtain new random values between runs of the same code; the current time is a good seed. The following code uses this and then prints nine random numbers in a loop:

```
random/seed now/time
loop 9 [
    r: random 10
    prin r prin space
]                         ;1st run: == 4 5 3 5 7 9 3 10 10
                          ;2nd run: == 10 8 10 2 3 1 4 2 1
```

Order of evaluation

You will know from other programming languages that a strict, so-called *precedence order* is followed to determine the order that operations are evaluated in expressions. Sometimes, you need to consult the precedence table to be sure, or use parentheses to indicate the evaluation order.

In Red, you can and should also use parentheses for the same reason, but otherwise expressions are *evaluated from left to right*, as shown here:

```
1 + 2 * 3   ;== 9     ; other languages would return 7!
1 + (2 * 3) ;== 7     ; use ( ) to get that result in Red
```

Another way to enforce the common evaluation order is to put the expression inside a block and use the `math` function:

```
math  [1 + 2 * 3]    ;== 7
```

To get a better feeling for this, let's examine a more complicated expression:

```
print 10 + sine 30 + 60      ;== 11.0
```

This is evaluated as follows:

```
print (10 + sine 30 + 60)      (1.)
print (10 + (sine 30 + 60))    (2.)
print (10 + (sine (30 + 60)))  (3.)
print (10 + (sine (90)))       (4.)
```

Let's understand each step:

1. `print` accepts one argument
2. The arguments for the left + are found to the left and right side of it:
   - The first argument for + is `10`
   - The second argument is a function called `sine`

3. `sine` takes one argument, which is another addition of two numbers, so the input to `sine` is 90—sine90 gives `1.0`
4. So the result is `11.0`

You could also view it like this:

```
print
    10
    +
    sine
        30
        +
        60
```

So, from left to right, look at the function and determine how many arguments it needs. The argument(s) themselves can contain functions that must be evaluated first using the same rule, and going from right to left. When several things have to be evaluated one after another, Red always *returns the last value*.

⇒ Now answer question 11 from the *Questions* section.

Evaluation with do and reduce

In the previous chapter, we saw how to use do to evaluate a script in the console with do %script.red.

In fact, do is more general in that it accepts any expression, function, or block, such as here:

```
;-- see Chapter03/evaluating.red:
do 9 * 9                        ;== 81
do square-root 25               ;== 5.0
do [print [tab uppercase "Red"]] ; == "RED"
```

You can even use do %script.red *from inside a Red program*, that's how powerful it is. Let's make script.red containing—Red[] print "This is executed in a script". Now edit an evaluating.red program containing—Red[] do %script.red.

Then red evaluating.red will print the text, This is executed in a script in the console. To see the same output in a terminal compile it with red -r evaluating.red and then type the command ./evaluating.

The reduce word evaluates expressions inside a block and returns a new block with the evaluated values, such as in this example:

```
bl: [8 * 3 99 / 11 square-root 25 [pi ** 2]]
r: reduce bl            ;== [24 9 5.0 [pi ** 2]]
bl                      ;== [8 * 3 99 / 11 square-root 25 [pi ** 2]]
```

You see that reduce does not evaluate nested blocks, and the original block remains unchanged.

The structure of a Red program

Until now, we have mostly used snippets of code, but a complete Red program starts with a Red [] block, called its *header*. If this is not present, the compilation stops immediately with the following message:

```
*** Syntax Error: Invalid Red program
```

Why is it needed? It must be there to signal that the file contains a script and not just random text; in fact, the .red extension is not at all needed for the compiler to work.

An empty header, such as the one we used, is not usually a good idea. In fact, the header is an *information block* that can contain all kinds of (meta)-info and documentation about the program, in the form of a series of pairs enclosed between rectangular brackets [ ]:

```
Red [
    Name-Of-Info: "Value of Info"
    Name-Of-Info2: "Value of Info2"
    ...
]
```

The header provides information to you and other developers, and also to documentation tools that could extract this info. The values can be of any type, not just strings.

Here is a fairly complete example:

```
;-- see Chapter03/template.red:
Red [
    title: "template script"
    author: "Ivo Balbaert"
    date: 2018-02-10
    file: %template.red
    tabs: 4
    version: 1.0
    company: ""
    rights: "Copyright (C) 2018 Ivo Balbaert. All rights reserved."
    license: {
        Distributed under the Boost Software License, Version 1.0.
        See https://github.com/red/red/blob/master/BSL-License.txt
    }
    summary: { Purpose of program }
]
```

An *icon* header can be used to change the default app icon by declaring it here, but make sure you have your new `.ico` file in the folder.

Other possible info-items are—*Date, Description, Comments, Note,* and *History*. In fact, you could invent your own items. Generally speaking, the following seem the most useful—*Author, Date, Version, Description, History, Company*. In fact, none of these info-items is mandatory, but when a special dialect is needed in the program, this must be signaled to the compiler by including a *needs* header, for example, for the graphical interface `view` dialect (see `Chapter 9`, *Composing Visual Interfaces* and `Chapter 10`, *Advanced Red*):

```
Red [needs: 'view]
```

⇒ Now answer question 12 from the *Questions* section.

A program starts executing the first line after the header where executable code is found. There is no `main` function or anything like that in Red—execution goes on sequentially, line by line.

Indentation in a Red script is used to provide more structured and readable code—use a *four-spaces indent per level*, don't use tabs (let your editor convert them to spaces!). Visual Studio Code warns you of faulty indentation by showing them with a red margin.

Summary

In this chapter, we learned how to define variables and how to examine them. We also got a better understanding of how Red works with types, and of the structure of a Red program.

In the following chapter, we will start writing real programs by examining how to control the flow and how to repeat pieces of code.

Questions

1. What's wrong with the following line of code? Correct it:

   ```
   name: John
   ```

2. Examine the `system` word in the console with `? system`.
3. Give the values of `i1` and `i2` after evaluating `i2: 1 + i1: 1`.
4. To better see the difference between them, use `print` and `probe` on `[10 * 5]`.
5. Coming from other languages, it is common to type the mistake `to_float 42;` what happens then? Explain this.
6. See whether you can find the results of the following expressions for yourself (see `Chapter03/evaluation.red`):

   ```
   print (6 < 13) and (42 < 33)
   print (43 < 42) xor (44 < 43)
   print complement 3
   ```

7. From the following code snippet evaluate the last three lines and explain the results:

```
a: "red" ;== "red"
b: copy a ;== "red"
a = b
a == b
a =? b
```

8. What's the output of `print [3 = 2 tab 5 = 5 tab 1 = 1.0]`?

9. What is the output of `on = (5 = 5)`?

10. Look up the docs of `now` in the console and try out its refinements.

11. Why does `square-root 9 + square-root 9` return `3.464101615137754` and not `6`? Make it return `6.0`.

12. Compile a `minimal.red` script with only a header. What is the size of the binary? Use –c and –r, is there a difference, and if so, why?

Further reading

A more detailed discussion, written by André Ungaretti, on the evaluation order with numerous examples can be found here: `http://helpin.red/`.

4
Code-Controlling Structures

In this chapter, you will learn how to create more complex code by adding conditions, selections, and loop structures. We will also show you how to do error handling in Red. This is illustrated throughout the chapter through the development of a guessing game, in which the user must guess a secret number between 1 and 99. That secret number is randomly generated in the program.

To do this, we need to learn how to get data into a Red program and how to test this input. We need to do this a number of times until the right number is guessed. Overall, we need to make sure our program can deal with the wrong kinds of input.

In this chapter, we will cover the following topics:

- Getting input from the user
- Testing conditions
- Structuring repetitions
- The number-guessing game
- Handling errors
- Creating and catching errors

Technical requirements

You'll find the code for this chapter at `https://github.com/PacktPublishing/Learn-Red-Fundamentals-of-Red/tree/master/Chapter04`. If you have installed Red as indicated in `Chapter 2`, *Setting Up for Development*, you are good to go. You can work on Windows, macOS X, or Linux. You can type or paste any code in the Red console to see its results, or you can start using an editor, such as Visual Studio Code.

Getting input from the user – input and ask

The easiest way to get an input is to use the `input` word, as shown in the following code snippet:

```
;-- see Chapter04/getting-input.red:
print "Enter a number: "
num: input
print ["You entered the number" num "with" length? num "digits"]
```

When interpreted with the console through `red getting-input.red` or from within the console with `do %getting-input.red`, we get the following result when the number `89` is entered:

```
Enter a number:
89
You entered the number 89 with 2 digits
```

What is the datatype of `num`? If we try `length? 89` in the console, we get a `*** Script Error: length? does not allow integer! for its series` argument. But `length? "89"` returns 2, so `num` must be of a `string!` type. Indeed, anything typed into the console is received by Red as a string. This is so for the `input` word, and also for the `ask` word, which we'll use shortly.

What if we want to *compile* this little program with `red -r` or `red -c`? This gives you a `*** Compilation Error: undefined word` input. The reason for this is that the `input` word is not yet compiled into the standard library (this will probably change in the future). For now, in order to compile this, you have to include the source code for `input`. This is done by using the following line, just after the Red header:

```
#include %../../../red-source/environment/console/CLI/input.red
```

The file we need is `input.red`, in which `input` and other words are defined. This file is included in Red's source code in the `environment/console/CLI` folder. If you haven't yet downloaded the source code, do so now and place it in a folder named `red-source` (see the *A look at the source code* section in `Chapter 2`, *Setting Up for Development*). This workaround should no longer be necessary from v 0.6.4 onward.

To include a source file in another Red file, use the `#include` command. Because this needs a file, its argument starts with a `%` sign.

> The `#include` word is used when you want to import a Red script. It makes the functions in the included file available. It is, in fact, nothing more than a copy and paste of the code—it does not execute that code. This is in contrast to `do %file.red`, which does the same as `#include` and then executes the code.

What is the `../` for? This is just to indicate to jump a folder up in the directory structure, where our `getting-input.red` file is located; it is a relative path. In my case, I had to jump up three folder levels; for you, this could be different. This `#include` in turn will include a number of other files from the `/environment/console` directory (look at the source of `input.red`).

With this in place, a `red -r` compilation will give you an executable that has the aforementioned behavior when run with `./getting-input`.

The `ask` word allows us to display a string while *asking*, effectively replacing the `print` and `input`:

```
;-- see Chapter04/ask-input.red:
num: ask "Enter a number: "
print ["You entered the number" num "with" length? num "digits"]
```

When compiling, you again need to use the `#include` word, because `ask` is not yet included in the standard compilation procedure. You should also use the `red -r` command.

> To keep a Red program open and waiting for input, use `ask ""` as the last line in your script, as follows:
> ```
> ask "Enter some text: "
> ask ""
> ```
> An alternative is to start your Red script with the following options:
> ```
> red --cli --catch
> ```

What we get from `ask` and `input` is a string with the newline character removed; the `length?` word gives you the number of characters. In order to get the integer equivalent, we can use `to-integer` or `load` from the previous chapter. So now we have learned how to ask the user for a number guess.

Testing conditions

How can we execute a different branch of code depending on a condition? For instance, in our game, we will have to test whether the input number is bigger or smaller than the number to be guessed. Red gives us different ways to do this.

if

Here is how `if` works:

- When a condition is true, then evaluate the block of code that follows
- If the condition is false, do nothing; more precisely, the `none` value is returned:

```
;-- see Chapter04/conditions.red:
account: -250
if account < 0 [print "Your account is overdrawn."] ;== Your
account is overdrawn.
if now/time < 12:00 [print "before noon"]            ;== before
noon, if e.g. 10:53
```

The condition (here, `account < 0` or `now/time < 12:00`) need *not* be enclosed in ( ), but the code following it must be in a block `[]`.

Logical operations such as `and`, `or`, and `not` can be used to create composite conditions. For instance, here we use `not` to test whether a file is present, using the `exists?` function:

```
if not exists? %missing.txt [print "File missing.txt does not exist"]
```

If you don't have this file in your folder, the message is printed.

We can also use `any` or `all`:

```
n: 12    m: 42
if any [n = 13 m = 42] [print "true!"]       ;== true!
if all [n = 13 m = 42] [print "true!"]       ;== none
; nothing is printed and none is returned because not all expressions are
true
```

It is important to note that Red considers everything that is not `false` or `none` to be true:

```
if 42    [print "true!"]    ; == true!
if "ok"  [print "true!"]    ; == true!
if 0     [print "true!"]    ; == true!
if []    [print "true!"]    ; == true!
if none  [print "true!"]    ; == none
if false [print "true!"]    ; == none
```

=> Now answer question 1 in the *Questions* section.

unless

Red also has an `unless` word, which is the same as `if not`.

The block after `unless` is executed only if the condition is `false`. So we could have written the preceding line with the file existence test as the following:

```
unless exists? %missing.txt [print "File missing.txt does not exist"]
```

either

What is the result of the following line?

```
if 13 < 42 [print "13 < 42"] [print "13 > 42"]
; 13 < 42  ; == [print "13 > 42"]
```

As you can see, it prints out `13 < 42` correctly, but the return value is the following:

```
[print "13 > 42"]
```

This is normal behavior—this block comes after the `if`, so it is returned as a block.

In contrast to most other programming languages, the `if` in Red *does not have an* `else` *branch,* so be aware of this behavior!

If you need an `if...else` structure, use `either`. So for the preceding statement, use the following:

```
either 13 < 42 [print "13 < 42"][print "13 > 42"]    ; == 13 < 42
```

This puts out the expected result of 13 < 42. The other branch is used when we use >instead of <:

```
either 13 > 42 [print "13 > 42"][print "13 < 42"]    ;== 13 < 42
```

 Remember, if takes only one block, either must have two blocks!

Here is another example:

```
print either now/time < 12:00 ["AM"]["PM"]    ;== PM
```

The now/time phrase gives you the current time, which prints out PM when the time is 16:23, for example.

Of course, the blocks can also contain binding statements:

```
n: 42
either n < 0 [msg: "negative"][msg: "zero or positive"]
print ["n is" msg]    ;== n is zero or positive
```

When both branches return a value of the same type, as is the case here, the result of either can be bound to a word, as shown in the following code:

```
n: 42
msg: either n < 0 ["negative"]["zero or positive"] ;== "zero or positive"
msg    ;== "zero or positive"
```

Where blocks contain multiple statements, you should use the following style with an indentation of four spaces. This is illustrated in the following code snippet, which simulates a user login action:

```
user: ask "Username (jvh38): "
pass: ask "Password (avi108): "
either all [user = "jvh38" pass = "avi108"][
    print ["Hi" user]
    print "Welcome back"
][
    print "Incorrect Username/Password"
]
;-- if input entered as shown:
;== Hi jvh38
;== Welcome back
```

Use this as the standard way to write blocks on multiple lines. The `either` blocks can also be nested inside each other, but this quickly becomes difficult to read, so don't overuse this.

=> Now answer questions 2 and 3 in the *Questions* section.

Stopping a program – halt or quit

How do you stop a program when a certain condition is met? For example, in our guessing program, we want to stop running the script when the user enters the letter S. Here is the solution—just use `quit` in the console, as shown in the following code:

```
answer: ask "Type a number (from 1 till 99) or stop(S): "
if answer = "S" [
    print "OK, you want to stop."
    quit
]
print "This line is not executed when S is entered"
```

This could be written as an `either` statement, but I find it more readable in this format.

The `quit` word can also be used to exit from a program when there is an error condition.

With the `/return` refinement, you can signal a return status to the operating system by phrasing it as `quit/return` 5. You could also use the alternative phrase `-return` 5. This can be useful when the Red program is called from a shell script.

If your program is interpreted rather than compiled, you can use `halt` instead of `quit`. This will return control to the Red console prompt instead of to the operating system level, and `(halted)` will be displayed. For example:

```
if now/time > 19:00 [prin "Stop working" halt]     ;== Stop working(halted)
```

If you need to pause a running script for a certain amount of time, say, five seconds, use `wait 5`.

switch and case

Suppose you have to test different *values* of a word, and each value requires a different action. How would you do it? You could use multiple `if` tests, phrased as `if var = value1`, but then you would have to add a new `if` for each new value to be tested, and all `if` tests would then be executed. Red has a versatile `switch` word, which allows you to do just that, but in one statement. For example:

```
person: "John"
switch person [
    "Bob"   [print "Bob is at the gym"]
    "John"  [print "John is at work"]
    "Laila" [print "Laila is shopping"]
] ;== John is at work
```

The `switch` word evaluates the `person` word, and executes only the branch that corresponds to the same value.

If the value is not found, no branch is executed. In that case, it might be useful to provide a default branch with the refinement `/default`, as shown in the following code:

```
person: "John"
switch/default person [
    "Bob"      [print "Bob is at the gym"]
    "Lawrence" [print "Lawrence is at work"]
    "Laila"    [print "Laila is shopping"]
][
    print "person not found"
] ;== person not found
```

The word to be tested can be of any datatype, including numbers, strings, words, dates, times, URLs, files, and blocks. You can even test the type of a word, as shown in the following code:

```
var: 108
switch type?/word var [
    string!  [print "found a string"]
    binary!  [print "found a binary"]
    integer! [print "found an integer number"]
    decimal! [print "found a decimal number"]
]   ;== found an integer number
```

The `switch` values can also be of a different datatype.

=> Now answer question 4 in the *Questions* section.

Instead of testing values, can we also test *conditionals*? Again, you could do this with several `if` statements, but a better approach is to use `case`, which evaluates a number of conditions. The block of the first condition that is `true` is evaluated, as shown here:

```
num: 42
case [
    num > 42 [print "num is more than 42"]
    num < 42 [print "num is less than 42"]
    num > 33 [print "num is more than 33"]
    num = 42 [print "num is 42"]
    true     [print "yes its true"]
] ;== num is more than 33
```

Only one block is executed. If you want all blocks whose conditions are true to be evaluated, use the `/all` refinement. If we replace `case` with `case/all` in the preceding example, the output is as follows:

```
num is more than 33
num is 42
yes its true
```

The `true` branch is the default branch, but it is optional. Use `case` when you have to choose between a variety of actions, depending on the situation.

=> Now answer question 5 in the *Questions* section.

catch and throw

Another mechanism that allows for code control is `catch – throw`. Have a look at the following example:

```
catch [
    print "before throw"
    throw "error"
    print "after throw"
]
```

This prints `before throw` and returns `error`. The `throw` word interrupts the code flow and goes back to the next higher level `catch`, returning the value given by `throw`. `catch` must always be followed by a block `[ ... ]` containing statements or a function call.

While `case` can only be used in a local block with all possible conditions specified, `catch` can be used when calling a function, that contains a `throw`, like this:

```
catch [ function-name arguments]
```

`catch / throw` works across function boundaries—a `throw` occurring in a nested function can be caught at a higher function level.

You can't use `throw` without `catch`, as you can see with `if n = 0 [throw 5]`, which gives us the error `*** Throw Error: no catch for throw: 5`.

To obtain more possibilities, `throw` can have a `/name` refinement, phrased as `throw/name rvalue tname`, where `tname` is the `throw` name and `rvalue` is the return value. These `throw` words are still caught by `catch`, but you can refine the catching by specifying one or more names with `catch`:

```
catch/name [some function call with a throw] 'tname
```

Here, `tname` can also be a block, such as `[tname1 tname2]`, to catch multiple named instances of `throw`.

An elaborate example of using catch and throw with functions and names can be found here: `http://www.red-by-example.org/#catch`.

Although `catch throw` looks a lot like an error-handling structure such as those used in other languages, it really isn't! Errors occur during execution (at runtime), without being intended by the programmer. The `catch` and `throw` words are deliberately programmed. For error handling, use the techniques described in the *Handling errors* section.

Structuring repetitions

Often, you need to repeat a block of code lines, either a number of times or while a certain condition holds true. The `forever` word lets you repeat an unlimited number of times. This should be used with caution—be sure to use `break` to get out of the infinite loop and continue with the rest of the program. The following snippet shows the life of a fervent book reader:

```
;-- see Chapter04/repetitions.red:
count: 99
forever [
```

```
      print append form count " books to read"
      ; print [form count " books to read"]    ;-- same as append
      count: count - 1
      if count = 0 [break]
  ]
  ;== 99 books to read
  ;...
  ;== 2 books to read
  ;== 1 books to read
```

We break out of the loop when the count down reaches 0.

We use append to join two strings together—the first is form count (which converts count to a string), and the second string is the rest of the sentence. Instead of append, we could also just have used print [form count " books to read"].

Repeating a number of times – loop or repeat

If you need to execute a block a fixed number of times, the simplest way to do this is with loop:

```
  n: 3 ;== 3
  loop n [prin "looping "] ;= looping looping looping ; recall: prin is no
  newline
```

In loop, you can't use the counter in the code block. If you need to do that, use repeat:

```
  repeat i 5 [prin i]              ;== 12345
```

The repeat word has an index (here named i) that gets incremented automatically each time round the loop. The index counts from 1 to the second argument, which is the number of cycles. You can use and change i in the code block itself, but i is reinitialized at the beginning of each loop, as you can see in the following code:

```
  repeat i 5 [i: i + 2 prin i]    ;== 34567
```

=> Now answer question 6 from the *Questions* section.

Repeating with a condition – while or until

On other occasions, you might want the loop continuations to depend on a condition:

- You may want to continue `while` a certain condition is true, and stop with the loop when the condition turns false

- You may want to do the opposite—loop `until` a certain condition is true

Here is an example of the `while` word, printing out the odd integers smaller than `10`:

```
n: 1
while [n <= 10 ][
    if odd? n [prin n prin " "]
    n: n + 1
] ;== 1 3 5 7 9
```

Note that the condition (here, `n <= 10`) must be in a code block, `[ ]`. This block may contain multiple statements and expressions; the last one is taken as a condition.

We can have the same result by simulating a second step:

```
n: 1
while [n <= 10 ][
    prin n prin " "
    n: n + 2
] ;== 1 3 5 7 9
```

Every `while` can be turned into an `until` by inverting the condition. But be careful—the condition, that should become true at a certain moment, must appear as *the last expression in the* `until` *block*:

```
n: 1
until [
    prin n prin " "
    n: n + 2
    n > 10 ; the condition to end the loop
] ;== 1 3 5 7 9
```

This also means that the block will be executed at least once.

The `break` word can be used to break out of any kind of loop. If it's useful, you can return a value with `break/return value`. If you want to skip the current iteration of the loop, use `continue` to transfer control back to the start of the loop to begin the next iteration. The following code snippet illustrates this:

```
repeat n 8 [
    prin ["Before" n " - "]
    if n < 3 [continue]
    if n = 6 [break]
    prin ["After" n " - "]
]
```

This prints out the following:

```
Before 1 - Before 2 - Before 3 - After 3 - Before 4 - After 4 -
Before 5 - After 5 - Before 6 -
```

 There is no `for` word in Red to do something like `for i = 2 to 10 step 2`, as would be done in other languages. Instead, use `repeat` and `while` to accomplish what you want. For example, the `to value` phrase can be used with a `<= value` condition in `while`, and a step can be performed in the `while` code block with `i: i + step`.

When looping through a series in a block, you'll most often use `foreach` and `forall`, which we'll discuss in the next chapter.

=> Now answer question 7 from the *Questions* section.

A number-guessing game

Now we have all the building blocks needed for our game.

From the previous chapter, we already know how to pick a random number between 1 and 99, and how to seed this so that each time, the program gives another `secret-number`:

```
;-- see Chapter04/guess-number.red:
random/seed now/time
secret-number: random 99
```

Getting input from the user is done with `ask`; we saw a code snippet for this in the *Stopping a program* section. The user is allowed to guess a certain number of times, say, 10 times, and this number is stored in `max-number-of-guesses`. So all the code with its input and further logic must be executed in a loop with that particular number of iterations:

```
loop max-number-of-guesses [ code ]
```

We also keep track of the `number-of-guesses`. Of course, our program has to give a clear message at each step.

What are the logical steps each loop iteration has to go through? Let's note them down:

1. Take the input and check whether the user wants to stop.
2. Increment `number-of-guesses`, and check that we haven't yet exceeded the maximum number of guesses; if so, `break` from the loop.
3. Convert the input to a number to get `guessed-number`.
4. If `guessed-number` is the same as `secret-number`, the user has won the game. In this case, `break` from the loop.
5. Compare `guessed-number` to `secret-number`, and tell the user if their guess is bigger or smaller than the secret number. Then `continue`.

With everything explained, it is now easy to follow the complete code (see `guess-number.red`). We have omitted the header for the sake of brevity. The steps are indicated in the code, phrased as, for example, `;--2`:

```
random/seed now/time
secret-number: random 99
max-number-of-guesses: 10
number-of-guesses: 0

loop max-number-of-guesses [
;-- 1
    answer: ask "Type a number (from 1 till 99) or stop(S): "
    if answer = "S" [
        print "Allright, you want to stop."
        break
    ]
;-- 2
    number-of-guesses: number-of-guesses + 1
    print ["--> Number of guesses:" number-of-guesses]
    if number-of-guesses > (max-number-of-guesses - 1) [
        print ["Sorry, too much guessing, the secret number was"
    secret-number]
        break
```

```
        ]

        guessed-number: load answer ;-- 3
    ;-- 4
        if secret-number = guessed-number [
            print ["Congratulations. You guessed the number" secret-number
    "in" number-of-guesses "times"]
            break
        ]
    ;-- 5
        either secret-number < guessed-number [
            print ["The secret number is smaller than" guessed-number]
            continue
        ][
            print ["The secret number is bigger than" guessed-number]
            continue
        ]
    ] ; end loop

    print "Thanks for guessing!"
```

Compile the program with `red -r guess-number.red` and enjoy playing the game with `./guess-number`! Perhaps you can add some additional logic, such as the following:

- Notifying the user of the number of guesses that they have left after five attempts
- When the difference between the guess and the secret number is less than 10, telling the user that they are getting close

Do send a pull request to the GitHub repository!

Handling errors

Errors can be caused by wrong input from the user or they can be produced by the system.

If you enter `4 / 0` in the REPL, you will get a `*** Math Error: attempt to divide by zero` alert. The Red console does not crash in the case of an error, but a compiled program will.

The different types of predefined errors can be found with ?
`system/catalog/errors`.

To see the specific errors, use the type as a refinement—for example,
`? system/catalog/errors/syntax`, which shows, for example, a `no-`
`header`, `missing`, or `invalid` error.

Now, let's return to our guessing game. What happens if the user enters a string such
as `"abc"` instead of a number? Then the guessing stops right there—the program crashes
with the error:

```
;-- see Chapter04/handling-errors.red:
*** Script Error: cannot compare 4 with "abc"
*** Where: <
```

This occurs when comparing the secret number (in this case, 4) with the string `4 < "abc"`.

Red has different ways to make your program resilient against runtime errors that are
caused by dangerous input.

attempt and try

First, you can evaluate the dangerous code in a block with `attempt`:

```
attempt [4 < "abc"] ;== none
```

Instead of crashing with an error, this simply returns `none`, while well-behaving code
simply executes and returns its result, such as `attempt [4 * 7]     ;== 28`.

Because `attempt` effectively discards the error, this is not suitable for production code.
However, while developing, this can be used to flesh out the program's logic. Handling
errors is best done in a second phase, but then you should definitely use something better
than `attempt`, namely `try`.

The `try` word tries to evaluate a block, similar to `do`:

```
try [4 * 7]       ;== 28 ; normal evaluation result
try [4 / 0]       ; *** Math Error: attempt to divide by zero
type? try [4 / 0] ; == error!
```

We see that in the case of an error, `try` returns a value of the `error!` type.

The `try` word has a `/all` refinement that functions as an ultimate barrier; it catches all possible exceptions, including inappropriate uses of `break` and `continue`, and also of `return` or `exit`, which we'll encounter in `Chapter 6`, *Using Functions and Objects*.

Using error?

Use the type-test `error?` function in combination with `try` to test whether the code returns an error:

```
error? try [4 < "abc"]  ;== true
```

The `error? try` phrase returns `true` in the case of an error and `false` otherwise.

Don't forget that `try` is followed by the code block that must be tested. If you use `error?` without it, the dangerous code is not executed, so no `error!` is generated, returning `error? [4 < "abc"]  ;== false`.

We could use this to see if there is a runtime error with a condition test, phrased as `if error?try`:

```
if error? try [4 < "abc"][
    print "Wrong input, enter an integer!"
    quit ; or: continue
]
```

We could also use `either error? try`:

```
either error? try [4 < "abc"][
    print "Wrong input, enter an integer!"
    quit ; or: continue
][
    ; everything ok, now we can proceed
]
```

You can find out more details about an error that occurred with the `probe` word:

```
if error? err: try [4 < "abc"] [probe err]
```

This produces the following output, which is useful when debugging:

```
make error! [
    code: 339
    type: 'script
```

```
        id: 'invalid-compare
        arg1: 4
        arg2: "abc"
        arg3: none
        near: none
        where: '<
        stack: 77629472
]
*** Script Error: cannot compare 4 with "abc"
*** Where: <
*** Stack: probe
```

Creating and catching errors

In a situation where you know a runtime error could occur, you can invoke a specific error yourself by using `cause-error`. For example:

```
m: 10
if n = 0 [ cause-error 'math 'zero-divide [] ]
print m / n
```

This line generates a `*** Math Error: attempt to divide by zero` when n is 0. This could be useful when entering a function with an n parameter that could be 0, and when we want to divide by n   in the function.

Note that it needs the literal words `'math` and `'zero-divide`, describing the error's type and name; the third argument is a parameter block, which can be empty. Instead of `cause-error`, you can also encounter `make error! [math zero-divide]` or even `make error! 400`. They all do the same—generate the error with that name or code.

 Only use `cause-error` if you want to stop your program displaying the error message.

So to summarize, use `try`, `if error?`, `cause-error`, and the `error!` object together for proper error handling in Red.

The catch – throw phrase is meant for controlling code flow, as we saw in the *Catch and throw* section of this chapter, not for error-handling.

Checking types

Writing code that terminates with a runtime error is rather unprofessional, so whenever possible, use code that does not create an error. In our game, you could test the type of guessed-number with the following:

```
if integer? guessed-number
```

If guessed-number was not an integer, use continue to ask for a next guess:

```
;-- see Chapter04/guess-number2.red:
if not integer? guessed-number [
    print ["This is no integer! Try again."]
    continue
]
```

You could also use the more complicated if (type? guessed-number) <> integer! here, but we strive to make things simpler in Red, remember?

To check whether a value is a number (integer or float), use **number?** value.

We'll come back to this subject in Chapter 6, *Using Functions and Objects*, to discuss error handling with functions.

Summary

We have learned a lot in this chapter! We now know how to get console input from the user. We have learned various ways to bend our code to respond to conditions with if, either, switch, case or catch, and throw. We also saw that repeating code can be made with forever, loop, repeat, while, and until. We discussed how to perform error handling with attempt, try, error?, and cause-error. Finally, we built a number-guessing game that makes use of most of these techniques.

By now, you should be able to write out a program's logic in simple scripts. In the following chapter, you will learn how to work with blocks and series, the foundational data structure in Red.

Questions

1. Give the results of the following statements. Do it in your head first, then verify it in the console:

```
if 0 [print "0 is true"]
if 13 = 13.0 [print "ok"]
if 13 == 13.0 [print "ok"]
```

2. What is the value of `out` after executing the following statements?

```
p: 7
out: either p == 7.0 ["p is 7"]["bad luck"]
```

3. Write a code snippet that asks the user whether it is raining, and provide the appropriate whether or not it is raining. Use the multiline block style.

4. Write a `switch` snippet where the values are of different datatypes—for example, use an `item` variable that has the `"red"` value and test on different values.

5. Write a `case` snippet that tests whether a `name` word contains a vowel (a, e, i, o, or u). Hint: The conditions are of the form `find name "a";`, and so on. Look up an explanation with `? find` in the REPL. We'll discuss `find` in the next chapter.

6. Write a loop that produces the output `1 2 3 4 5 6 7`. Hint: Use `append` and `form`, as in the `forever` loop.

7. Write a rocket countdown (from 10 to 1).

Working with Series and Blocks

5

As you know by now, nearly everything in Red gets written inside `[ ]`. These denote blocks, which are a kind of series. Blocks and series form the foundation of Red code; in fact, if you look at the type hierarchy in Chapter 3, *Using Words, Values, and Types*, a block is also a `series!` type. A `series!` type contains a lot of other common types besides blocks, such as strings, files, binary values, tags, emails, images, and so on. That's why the functions and actions that work with block series can be applied to other types of values. For example, strings are essentially series of characters, and so the techniques used to manipulate block series can also be used for string operations.

In this chapter, we will learn how to work with series. We'll learn how to view a series as something that has a head and a tail, and a moving index. We'll learn how to get information from a series, how to move through it, search, sort, and change it. These operations are the bread and butter of a Red developer, and mastering the use of series is a core skill required for attaining Red proficiency!

In this chapter, we will cover the following topics:

- Series and blocks
- Navigating and looping through a series
- Getting information from a series
- Changing a series
- Copying a series
- Strings as series

Technical requirements

You'll find the code for this chapter at `https://github.com/PacktPublishing/Learn-Red-Fundamentals-of-Red/tree/master/Chapter05`. If you have installed Red on Windows, OS X, or Linux, as indicated in `Chapter 2`, *Setting Up for Development*, you are good to go. You can type or paste any code in the Red console to see its results, or you can start using an editor, such as Visual Studio Code.

Series and blocks

Let's look at an example. The letters `A B C D` are contained within the block `[A B C D]`. Coming from other programming languages, you may be more used to terms such as *lists* or *arrays*. These are very much the same as series. In Red, multidimensional arrays can be represented by nested blocks. If you want a more formal definition, we could say that a series is *an ordered set of items*, which can be values (data) or words (code). In the preceding example, the items are words such as `A B` and so on (they are not strings or characters), and they must get a value at some time while running the program. In Red, you can manipulate code as easily as you can manipulate data.

=> Now answer question 1 from the *Questions* section.

Because a series is ordered, each item in it can be referred to by a number—its *index*. The index in Red starts counting from 1, so the item with index 3 in the preceding series is `C`. In the string series `"Good dog!"`, the index 4 item is the #`"d"` character. There is also the *empty series*, which has no elements—`[]` or `""`.

We can give our series a name—`data: [A B C D]`; its type is `block!`. But it is also a `series?`, if you look at the *type diagram* in *The type system* section in `Chapter 3`, *Using Words, Values, and Types*. This diagram also shows that `any-block?` is a subtype of `series?`:

```
type? data    ;== block!
block? data   ;== true
series? data  ;== true
```

Here are some more examples of series:

```
:-- see Chapter05/series-and-blocks.red:
names: ["John" "Dave" "Jane" "Bob" "Sue"]
codes: [2804 9439 2386 9823 4217]
files: [%employees %vendors %contractors %events]
sales: ["Saturday" 56 "Sunday" 11]
some-code: [print "Hello"]
```

Let's now see how to move within a series.

Navigating and looping through a series

Navigating through a series is not rocket science, but you have to get used to it. Follow along in the console, and, to really get it, draw some pictures, such as the ones we will show you.

A step at a time – head, tail, index?, and next

The `data` word from the previous section is not only a name for the series—it is also a pointer to where we are in the series at a particular moment. You could call that position the *current index,* which is given by the `index?` function. Right after the series is created, we have `index? data ;== 1` . Here is a diagram so you can quickly see what is going on:

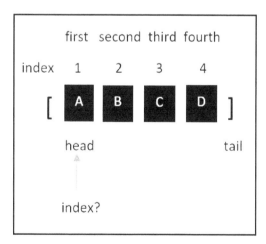

Remember that in Red, an index starts from 1, not from 0, as in most other (C-based) languages.

When the current index is 1, we are also at the *head* of the series:

```
;-- see Chapter05/navigating-and-looping.red:
head? data    ;== true
```

The `head data` phrase returns the whole [A B C D] series, starting from index 1. The tail always points just beyond the last element of a series, so now it's an empty list:

```
tail data ;== []
```

We are at the head, not at the tail, so `tail? data ;== false`. You can also ask for the `first`, `second` (and so on until the `fifth`) item of a series:

```
first data    ;== A
second data   ;== B
last data     ;== D
```

We can move forward through a series with the `next` action—for example, `next data ;== [B C D]`.

Now the current index has shifted one position to the right (the end) of the series.

The `data` word hasn't changed after `next`—it is still [A B C D]—so applying `next` several times won't change anything. If you want `data` to change, you must create a new binding. Instead of `next data`, do the following:

```
data: next data ;== [B C D]
data             ;== [B C D]
```

Here is a diagram to make it clear what has happened after `next`:

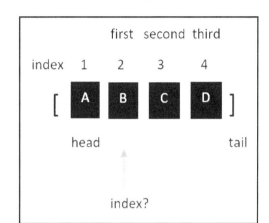

The `next` word increments the current index. `index? data` is now 2, `head? data` returns `false` (we're not at the head anymore, the tail functions give the same result, and `first data` is now B.

What happens when we get beyond the end of the series?

=> Find this out by answering question 2 from the *Questions* section.

We can see that `data` has become `[]` and `tail? data` now returns `true`. Perhaps surprisingly, `first data` returns `none` and `index? data` is 5—we simply moved beyond the series without getting an error.

You can also experiment in moving backwards in the series with the opposite effects by using `back`. To move through more steps at a time, use **skip** `data n`, where n is an integer giving the number of steps to take. Also, find out what happens when we use `data: skip data -2`.

=> Now try out questions 3 and 4 in the *Questions* section.

You may wonder where the complete series is. It is still intact in memory, right before you:

```
head data            ; == [A B C D]
```

To restart at the beginning of a series, simply use `head` and assign it to `data`:

```
data: head data      ; == [A B C D]
```

This is intentional—Red *reuses series* a lot to allow scripts to run faster and save memory.

Looping through a series – foreach and forall

In many cases, you'll want to go through an entire series, executing code for each item in the series, using something easier than `next`. Red has the `foreach` and `forall` words to do just that.

The `foreach` word executes a code block *for each item* in the series:

```
names: ["John" "Dave" "Jane"]
foreach name names [print name]
```

This prints out the following:

```
John
Dave
Jane
```

You should choose a descriptive word for the iteration variable (here, we have used `name`). It takes on the values of the items one by one, in order.

The `forall` word also moves through the series, but it executes a code block *for all the items together*, and combines this with a `next` at each iteration:

```
forall names [print names]
```

This then prints out the following:

```
John Dave Jane
Dave Jane
Jane
```

=> Now answer question 5 from the *Questions* section.

Suppose we have a series that we call `contacts` to store the names, addresses, and phones of my contacts, one on each line for readability:

```
contacts: [
    "John Smith" "123 Tomline Lane Forest Hills, NJ" "555-1234"
    "Paul Thompson" "234 Georgetown Pl. Grove, AL" "555-2345"
    "Jim Persee" "345 Pickles Pike Orange Grove, FL" "555-3456"
    "George Jones" "456 Topforge Court Mountain Creek, CO" ""
    "Tim Paulson" "" "555-5678"
]
```

A series is a straightforward way to structure data, with empty strings representing missing data.

The `foreach` word can do some very handy *pattern matching*, extracting items as desired:

```
foreach [name address phone] contacts [print [name "/" phone]]
```

This prints out the following:

```
John Smith / 555-1234
Paul Thompson / 555-2345
Jim Persee / 555-3456
George Jones /
Tim Paulson / 555-5678
```

The `while` or `repeat` loops from the previous chapter can always be used when you need more flexibility. For example:

```
colors: [red green blue yellow orange]
while [not tail? colors] [
    print first colors
    colors: next colors
]
```

This prints out the following:

```
red
green
blue
yellow
orange
```

Getting information from a series

A series can contain values of any type, even a mixture of types. It is often important to know how many items a series contains. This is given by the `length?` property:

```
;-- see Chapter05/getting-info.red:
data: [A B C D]
length? data ;== 4
```

If a series has no items, it is empty—the `empty?` function returns `true`:

```
empty-lst: []
length? empty-lst ;== 0
empty? empty-lst  ;== true
```

Selecting an item – pick and /

We can select an item in two ways, using our `data: [A B C D]` series:

- By specifying the item index in a so-called *path* notation, such as `data/3 ;== C`
- By specifying the item index with `pick`, such as **pick** `data 3 ;== C`

=> Now answer question 6 from the *Questions* section.

If the item index is a variable, here represented by `i`, you need to use the `:i` *get word* notation:

```
i: 3
data/:i      ;== C
data/(i)     ;== C   ; this alternative works also
```

 This is important to remember, because `data/i` doesn't give any error, but returns `none`. When the specified index is out of range, no error is generated, and the result is also `none`, for example, `pick data 100 ;== none`.

Strings are also series, so `pick` and / work for strings as well, with a character (#) as the result:

```
s: "I'm enjoying Red"
s/4          ;== #" "
pick s 5     ;== #"e"
```

It is important to note that for the `pick` and `/` functions, the given index starts counting from the current index `index?` value:
```
data: next data  ;== [B C D]
pick data 3      ;== D
data/3           ;== D
```

This `/` path notation is often used to do the following:

- To access items from nested *series* (see the *Changing items – poke, replace, and change* section)
- To get characters from strings with `pick`
- To access variables in *objects*, such as `system/console/prompt` (which is >>)
- To add refinements to *functions* to change how they work
- To describe the path to files and directories

The `a/b/c` phrase is an example of a path value:
```
type? 'a/b/c    ;== path!
```

The `path!` word is even a type in the type-system. Because paths are a type of series (see the type diagram in *The type system* section in `Chapter 3`, *Using Words, Values, and Types*), anything you can do with a series, you can also do with a path value. For example:
```
second system/console/prompt    ;== #">
```

⇒ Now try your hand at question 7 from the *Questions* section.

To quickly get part of a series starting from a given index, use `at`:
```
at data 3 ;== [C D]
```

Another handy operation is `extract`. This has an integer argument n, which allows you to get each `nth` item from the series, starting with the first item. Here, we use our previous `contacts` series to get the names only—**extract** `contacts` **3**.

This gives us the following result:
```
[
    "John Smith"
    "Paul Thompson"
    "Jim Persee"
    "George Jones"
    "Tim Paulson"
]
```

The rule is simple: Start at the first item, then count (including that item) to the given number, then take that item, and so on.

If you want to start from a certain position in the series—for example, to get only the phone numbers—specify this with a refinement, such as extract/index series n position:

```
phones: extract/index contacts 3 3
;== ["555-1234" "555-2345" "555-3456" "" "555-5678"]
```

Searching for an item – select and find

For searching for an item, there are two specific words—select and find. At first, their operation seems strange. The select word *returns the next item* from the series after the search match:

```
data1: [1 2 3 4]
select data1 2 ;== 3
select data1 99 ;== none
```

If the item is not found, none is returned. If the searched word has no value, use it as a block to prevent its evaluation or use it as a literal word with ':

```
data2: [A B C D]
select data2 [B]    ;== C
select data2 'B     ;== C
```

The find word, on the other hand, starts *at the match* and goes all the way to the tail, returning that part as a series:

```
find data1 2 ;== [2 3 4]
```

=> Now answer question 8 from the *Questions* section.

Both select and find have several refinements, which you can look up with ? select and ? find. Here, we will highlight a few important ones.

If you don't want to include the match with find, use /tail:

```
find/tail data1 2 ;== [3 4]
```

The /part word allows you to only search a part of the series, given by the number of items to search through:

```
blk: [11 12 13 14 [22 33 44] 15]
select blk 14          ;== [22 33 44]
select/part blk 12 3   ;== 13
select/part blk 14 3   ;== none
```

The following result may surprise you:

```
select blk [22 33 44] ;== none
```

The reason for this result is that, in order to search for a series *as a single value*, we must use the /only refinement, giving us the phrase select/only blk [22 33 44]   ;== 15.

The /only refinement is also used with many other words, with the same meaning.

Use /case when you need to do a case-sensitive search.

=> Now answer question 9 from the *Questions* section.

Sorting

In a lot of cases, searching is made faster by first *sorting* a series, as is done with sort:

```
codes: [2804 -9439 2386 9823 -4217]
sort codes                 ;== [-9439 -4217 2386 2804 9823]
codes                      ;== [-9439 -4217 2386 2804 9823]
sort/reverse codes         ;== == [9823 2804 2386 -4217 -9439]
```

Sorting happens in place, and the sorted codes series is also returned. The /reverse option sorts the series in descending order, from high to low. The sort word also accepts the /part refinement; using this word means that it will only sort that part of the series:

```
codes: [2804 -9439 2386 9823 -4217]
sort/part codes 4          ;== [-9439 2386 2804 9823 -4217]
```

Refinements can also be combined, as seen in the following code:

```
codes: [2804 -9439 2386 9823 -4217]
sort/reverse/part codes 4          ;== [9823 2804 2386 -9439 -4217]
```

To turn the order around (with the last item becoming first and so on), use reverse:

```
codes: [2804 -9439 2386 9823 -4217]
reverse codes
codes    ;== [-4217 9823 2386 -9439 2804]
```

The reverse word also changes the original series.

Changing a series

Now we will take a look at the action words that are dedicated to changing a series in one way or another—changing, adding, or deleting items.

Changing items – poke, replace, and change

There are two ways to change an item in a series. Let's use data: [A B C D], where A, B, C and D are all words. Suppose we want to replace C with the word X. We can do this as follows:

- Binding to a path specified by the item index—for example, data/3: 'X   ;== X. Now data has become [A B X D]. Why do we need 'X instead of just X? The reason is that when you're binding to a word, this word is evaluated. So you have to quote the X word in order to prevent evaluation. If you don't do this and use data/3: X, you'd get a **Script Error: X has no value.**
- Specifying the item index using poke, such as **poke** data 3 'X (the position comes first, then the new value).

(To replace C with the string "X" , we just have to use data/3: "X"   ;== "X"; then data becomes [A B "X" D]).

What if we want to change an item in a nested series, such as blk: [11 12 13 14 [22 33 44] 15] ? Suppose we want to change the 33 to 108. The easiest way is to use a path notation, such as blk/5/2: 108 (the nested series is item 5 in blk, and 33 is item 2 in the nested series). Now blk has indeed become [11 12 13 14 [22 108 44] 15].

Remember to use the get notation : when the indexes are words—for example, we can use `blk/:i/:j: 108` when i is 5 and j is 2.

=> Now answer question 10 from the *Questions* section.

Replacing an item in a series with something else is just as easy:

```
;-- see Chapter05/changing-series.red:
replace [10 11 12] 11 13 ;== [10 13 12]
```

Use `/all` if you need to replace all occurrences of a certain item:

```
replace/all [10 11 12 11] 11 13 ;== [10 13 12 13]
```

To change a number of items into other items at the current index of a series, use the `change` word:

```
s: [2 7 13 42]
change s [a b]      ;== [13 42]
s                   ;== [a b 13 42]
```

Other built-in words that can change series are `alter` and `swap`. See the codefile for some examples.

Adding new items – append, repend, and insert

To add new items to a series, you can use the `append`, `repend`, and `insert` words.

append

To add a new item *to the end of a series*, use the `append` word, which we have already encountered a few times:

```
append [10 11 12] 13       ;== [10 11 12 13]
append [10 11 12] [13 14]  ;== [10 11 12 13 14]
```

As you can see, the item to be added can also be a series, in which case it blends into the first series. If you want to add it as a series, you have to use `/only`:

```
append/only [10 11 12] [13 14]    ;== [10 11 12 [13 14]]
```

If you only want to add a limited number of items from a series, use `/part`:

```
append/part [10 11 12] [13 14 15] 2  ;== [10 11 12 13 14]
```

Find out what the `/dup` refinement is for using `?` and try it out!

Here is a more complete code snippet that illustrates the use of `append` with `foreach`, using safe initialization with `copy`:

```
list: ["John" 2804 "Dave" 9439 "Jane" 2386 "Bob" 9823 "Sue" 4217]
names: copy []
foreach [n c] list [append names n]   ; extract the names from list
names    ;== ["John" "Dave" "Jane" "Bob" "Sue"]
```

Here is another typical piece of code, using `repeat`, `length?`, and `append`:

```
names: ["John" "Dave" "Jane" "Bob" "Sue"]
repeat i (length? names) [
    print append append form i ": " pick names i
]
```

This prints the following as the output:

```
1: John
2: Dave
3: Jane
4: Bob
5: Sue
```

The code works as follows: `repeat` loops over the length of the series. For each item, you take its index `i`, which is made into a string with `form`. This is joined into a string with "`: `", making `append form i ": "`. This forms the first argument of the leftmost `append`; the second is `pick names i`, which is the name at that position, which in this case would be "`John`".

If this code does not read clearly to you, use temporary variables or parentheses to clarify:

```
names: ["John" "Dave" "Jane" "Bob" "Sue"]
repeat i (length? names) [
    print append (append form i ": ") (pick names i)
]
```

In general, to understand how a certain evaluation works, look up the documentation of the word (for example, append) with ? append in the REPL. From USAGE: APPEND series value, you can see that it takes two parameters. Then find these parameters, putting ( ) around each parameter that contains more than one word. In our example, this would give print append (append (form i) ": ") (pick names i). Then you can start removing superfluous instances of ( ), or giving a variable name to other parameters so that the parentheses are no longer needed.

Perhaps this sounded overly complex to you. We wanted to show you in detail how Red processes its syntax. But, in this case, you could just replace the line with the double append with this simple print block statement:

```
print [form i ":" pick names i]
```

repend

The repend word works in the same way as append, but repend first evaluates (or reduces—the re comes from reduce) the series to be added:

```
repend [10 11 12] [8 + 5 "pi"] ;== [10 11 12 13 "pi"]
```

As always, with /only, the added series stays a series:

```
repend/only [10 11 12] [8 + 5 "pi"] ;== == [10 11 12 [13 "pi"]]
```

insert

To add a new item into the series itself, use insert, which inserts the item at the current index (as you know, this is given by index? and can be changed by at). For a newly defined series, insert will occur at the start of the series:

```
s: [10 11 12]   ;== [10 11 12]
insert s 13     ;== [10 11 12]
s               ;== [13 10 11 12]
```

Here, you can see that insert returns the series after the insertion. But insert changes the series s as well so that you don't have to use s: insert s 13!

To specify the `insert` position, use `at`:

```
s: [10 11 12]      ; == [10 11 12]
insert at s 2 13   ; == [11 12]
s                  ; == [10 13 11 12]
```

The `insert` word has the same refinements as `append`.

Deleting items – remove and take

To delete the first item in a series, use `remove`:

```
remove [10 11 12] ; == [11 12]
```

The `take` word does the same, but returns that item instead of the changed series:

```
take [10 11 12] ; == 10
```

To delete an item at a certain position, use `at`, the same way as we did with `insert`:

```
s: [0 1 2 3 4 5]   ; == [0 1 2 3 4 5]
remove at s 2      ; == [2 3 4 5]
s                  ; == [0 2 3 4 5]   ; item 1 at position 2 is deleted
```

To delete the last item of a series, you could use `remove at s length? s`, but `take/last` does the same thing and returns that last item as well:

```
take/last [10 11 12] ; == 12
```

To delete a certain number of items, use `/part`:

```
remove/part [10 11 12] 2    ; == [12]
```

The `take/part` phrase has the same effect on a series, but returns the deleted items.

Eliminating duplicate items in a series is done with the `unique` word:

```
unique [7 13 42 108 2 7 14 42 109] returns [7 13 42 108 2 14 109]
```

If you need to remove each item in a series when it makes a certain condition true, use the
`remove-each` word, as in these examples:

```
ser: [7 13 42 108]
remove-each item ser [even? item]      ; (1)
ser   ;== [7 13]
remove-each item ser [item < 10]       ; (2)
ser   ;== [13]
```

As you can see, the condition is placed in a block. In line `(1)` all even numbers are
removed, in line `(2)` all numbers smaller than `10`.

All these functions change their series arguments!

Moving items – move and swap

To move the first item from one series to another, use the `move` word:

```
s: ["A" "B" "C"]
move [1 2 3] s      ;== [2 3]
s                   ;== [1 "A" "B" "C"]
```

It returns the changed first series, but, as you can see, the second series is also changed. To
move a number of items, use `/part` again in the code phrase `move/part series1
series2 number`.

=> Now answer question 11 from the *Questions* section.

Use `swap` to swap the first element(s) of two series. It returns the first series, but changes
both:

```
swap [A B C][1 2 3] ;== [1 B C]
```

Series as sets

Red has some basic operations to use so that it can work with series as sets. For example,
say we have two sets, s1 and s2, containing `s1: [7 13 42 108]` and `s2: [2 7 14 42
109]` (the code can be found in `Chapter05/sets.red`):

- `union s1 s2` returns `[7 13 42 108 2 14 109]`: the series are joined together,
  and duplicates are eliminated
- `intersect s1 s2` returns `[7 42]`: only the common elements are retained

- `difference s1 s2` returns [13 108 2 14 109]: only the elements that are not common to both are retained
- `exclude s1 s2` returns [13 108]: all elements from the second set are removed from the first set

Copying a series

Red tries to reuse series and objects in memory as much as possible, for performance reasons. This means that using variables to point to the same series is often a bad idea and is the cause of hard-to-find bugs in your code. We have already told you in the *Assigning and copying* section in Chapter 3, *Using Words, Values, and Types*, that using `copy` is the safest way to ensure that your variables point to different memory locations. That way, changes to one variable don't affect the other.

To appreciate this fact, examine and try to predict the output of the following code:

```
;-- see Chapter05/copying.red:
not-expected: [
    var1: ""
    append var1 "*"
    print var1
]

loop 3 [do not-expected]
```

The `do` word executes the `not-expected` code block and `append` joins the `var1` string with a `*`.

You probably expected three `*` lines to be printed out. But the actual output is the following:

```
*
**
***
```

Why is this? Because `var1` is a string, and so is a series, and it keeps its value in memory!

The `var1: ""` phrase is not an initialization as in most other programming languages—it is a binding, and the value to which the `var1` word is bound does not get erased by it.

In fact, this is what happens with `var1:  ""`:

1. New memory storage is allocated
2. That storage is initialized to an empty string
3. Then that storage is permanently assigned to the `var1` variable

The result we saw could be applied to a function to implement a local cache.

But if you don't want that, then what is the solution? Simply use a `copy  ""` phrase to do a proper initialization!

```
expected: [
    var1: copy ""
    append var1 "*"
    print var1
]

loop 3 [do expected]
```

The output produced is one * on three consecutive lines, as expected.

> The `copy` word effectively *copies the data* contained in series, strings, or other objects, and should almost always be used for such values. To create an empty block, use the following:
> `copy []`
> To create an empty string, use the following:
> `copy ""`

You may find this strange at this point, but persistent series are essential to the way Red works, and they enable many other valuable features in the language.

For the same reason, the safest way to delete all items in a series (starting from the current index) is to use the built-in action word `clear`:

```
data: [A B C D]
clear data
data  ;== []
```

If you want to copy only part of a value, use the /part refinement:

```
copy/part "Red herring" 3   ;== "Red"
copy/part [A B C D] 3        ;== [A B C]
```

The copy word we used until now is sometimes called *shallow copy*. Here is why:

```
nblk: [11 12 13 14 [22 33 44] 15]
blk: copy nblk    ;== [11 12 13 14 [22 33 44] 15]
nblk/3: 108
nblk              ;== [11 12 108 14 [22 33 44] 15]
blk               ;== [11 12 13 14 [22 33 44] 15]
```

The copied blk series is not changed when the original series changes—that's what we expect. But now look at what happens when we change something in the nested series:

```
nblk/5/2: 108
nblk    ;== [11 12 108 14 [22 108 44] 15]
blk     ;== [11 12 13 14 [22 108 44] 15]
```

The copied blk block also shows the change! The copy is shallow because, for *nested series*, a reference to that series is still assigned so that its value is not copied and changes can occur in the copy.

To avoid this, however deep the nesting level is, you have to make a deep copy with the /deep refinement. Let's use this on the same example:

```
nblk: [11 12 13 14 [22 33 44] 15]
blk: copy/deep nblk   ;== [11 12 13 14 [22 33 44] 15]
nblk/3: 108
nblk                  ;== [11 12 108 14 [22 33 44] 15]
blk                   ;== [11 12 13 14 [22 33 44] 15]
nblk/5/2: 108
nblk                  ;== [11 12 108 14 [22 108 44] 15]
blk                   ;== [11 12 13 14 [22 33 44] 15]
```

Now blk doesn't change, whatever happens to the original series.

Strings as series

Because strings are series of characters, all of the functions we talked about in this chapter also work for strings. Here are some examples of their usage with strings that show more advanced possibilities, which also apply to files, URLs, tags, and emails:

```
str: "Red"      ;== "Red"
type? str       ;== string!
string? str     ;== true
series? str     ;== true
```

Splitting a string – split

You can split a string on spaces, or on other characters, or even on strings - all these are called the *delimiter*, and the result of the split is a series. Here are some examples of this:

```
;-- see Chapter05/strings-as-series.red:
s1: "The quick brown fox jumps over the lazy dog"
split s1 " " ;== ["The" "quick" "brown" "fox" "jumps" "over" "the" "lazy"
"dog"]
s2: "bracadabra"
split s2 "a" ;== ["br" "c" "d" "br"]
s3: "abracadabra"
split s3 "a" ;== ["" "br" "c" "d" "br"]
```

From the last line, you can see that if the string starts with the delimiter, the first split item that will be found is an empty string "". The split word is very useful in the analysis and processing of text files.

Turning a series into a string – form

A series can be turned into a string using form. We saw in Chapter 3, *Using Words, Values, and Types*, that form turns every value into a string. In the case of a series, it removes the brackets and adds spaces between the items:

```
s: ["Red" "world" 13 42 4 * 8 ["a" "bee" "cee"]]
form s          ;== "Red world 13 42 4 * 8 a bee cee"
form/part s 15  ;== "Red world 13 42" ; limits the number of characters to
take
```

The original series is not changed. The form word is useful in turning a bunch of data containing [ ] into text.

Rejoining a block – rejoin

In the *Evaluation with do and reduce* section in Chapter 3, *Using Words, Values, and Types*, we saw how reduce evaluates expressions within a block, returning that block. The rejoin word goes one step further—it not only reduces a block, but it also *joins the items in the block into a string* with no spaces in between them. It returns the rejoined item, but the original series is not changed. It's like form, but with evaluation. Here are some examples of this:

```
ser: ["Product is: " 7 * 42]
rejoin ser    ;== "Product is: 294"
ser           ;== ["Product is: " 7 * 42]
```

Because rejoin converts a block into a string, it is often used in output print statements, such as print rejoin [newline "Total Images: " count] .

Clearing part of a string – clear and trim

Let's say we want to delete all contents after "American" in the string s: "American politics". We can apply clear , to skip all characters before "politics", making the phrase clear skip s 8 Or we can let Red do the work with find, making the phrase clear find s " politics". In both cases, s becomes "American".

If you just want to remove spaces from a string, use trim. This method is very versatile, and can include a lot of refinements:

```
str: " No more war ! "
trim/head str        ;== "No more war ! "
trim/tail str        ;== "No more war !"
; trim str           ; same as both /head and /tail
trim/all str         ;== "Nomorewar!" ; removes all spaces
trim/with str "!"    ;== "Nomorewar"   ; removes a specific string
```

The trim word is very useful when processing input or text files.

Let's also mention the pad word here, which is like the opposite of trim. It adds spaces to the right of a string (with /left to the left), so that the number of characters and spaces equals the number given:

```
s: "Red"
pad s 5
s ;== "Red   "
pad/left s 7
s ;== "   Red   "
```

The `pad` word is useful for producing aligned output.

Adding to a string – append and insert

To insert something at the beginning of a string, use `insert`:

```
str: "painting"
insert str "beautiful "
str ;== "beautiful painting"
```

Here is how you can `insert` a substring into a string at a certain position:

```
str: "abcdefg"
insert at str 3 "ONE"      ;== "cdefg"
str ;== "abONEcdefg"
; the same can be done with:
insert find str "c" "ONE" ;== "cdefg"
str                       ;== "abONEcdefg"
```

Again, for readability, you could write `insert (find str "c") "ONE"`.

By now, you know how to use `append` to add something to the tail of a string, in other words, to concatenate two strings:

```
str: "Red"              ;== "Red"
append str "100"        ;== "Red100"
append str [1 0 0]      ;== "Red100100"
```

Note that, in the last example, a series is automatically converted to a string using `form`.

Other useful tricks

In this section, we will look at a collection of examples to give you some ideas of how to apply certain actions to strings.

Use `find` to *find characters or substrings* in a string. Remember that it returns a substring starting with the matched character or string:

```
s1: "The quick brown fox jumps over the lazy dog"
find s1 "fox"   ;== "fox jumps over the lazy dog"
```

Change one character in a `s:` `"abcde"` string using `poke s 3 #"S"`, so that `s` becomes `"abSde"`.

You could also do this with `replace`, making `replace s "c" "S" ;== "abSde"`.

To *get the left part* of a string, provide a character count, as used in the phrase `copy/part str n`:

```
str: "beautiful"
copy/part str 4    ;== "beau"
```

To *remove the left part of a string*, effectively changing the string, use `remove/part`, as used in the phrase `remove/part str 4 ;== "tiful"`.

Similarly, to *get the right part* (n characters) of a string, use `at tail str -3`, which in this case returns `"ful"`.

To *get a substring* (in other words, the middle part) from a string, starting at a certain position and for a specified length, `copy/part` and `at` will do the trick:

```
str: "mnopqrst"
copy/part at str 2 4 ;-- start at position 2, get 4 items
;== "nopq"
```

Remove all the vowels from a string with `exclude`:

```
exclude "The United Kingdom" "aeiou" ;== "Th ndKgm"
```

To convert strings to lower- or uppercase, use the following words:

```
str: "Red"
lowercase str          ;== "red"
uppercase str          ;== "RED"
lowercase/part str 1
str                    ;== "rED"
```

=> Now answer question 12 from the *Questions* section.

Summary

Congratulations! You are now able to work with the fundamental data structure of Red. You have learned the concept of a series in Red, with its `head`, `tail`, and `next` words that are used to move the index position in the series. We have seen how to select an item with `pick` or the `/` syntax, and how to search for an item with `find` and `select`, as well as how to change, add, delete, and move items. Finally, we saw how to `copy` the value of a series, and how to use the series actions on strings.

The number of words to use for working with series may seem a bit overwhelming at first, but they are frequently used in code, so they will become familiar soon. It will also become clear that combining these words can result in some powerful code.

Questions

1. How can you make the series `data: [A B C D]` into a series of characters? Is it by phrasing it as `data: ["A" "B" "C" "D"]`?

2. We now have a `data` series that contains `[B C D]`. Move to the tail by applying `next` three times, while binding `data` to the result. Get the info at each next stage with `head?`, `tail?`, and `index?`. Draw a schema.

3. Using the series from the end of the previous question, apply `back` with binding and get the info.

4. Find out what happens when we use `data: skip data -2`.

5. Given the series `[323 2498 94321 31 82`, print out the numbers bigger than 1,000.

6. What is the result when you select an item from an empty series?

7. Given the series `s: ["A" "B" [42.1 42.2 42.3] red]`, how can you get to item `42.2` with the path notation? Try the same with `pick`.

8. Given the `s` series from the previous question, what is the result of `length`? `find s "B"`?

9. Given the `ser` series with the value of `[[3 7] [13 42] [108 666]]`, what is the value of `ser/1/2`? How do you select item `108`? How do you change `666` to `999`?

10. What is the result of the following two expressions:

```
select/part ["Red" "Crystal" "Ruby" "Java" "Go" "Rust"] ["Java"] 4
find/part ["Red" "Crystal" "Ruby" "Java" "Go" "Rust"] ["Java"] 4
```

What happens if you change 4 to 3?

11. Use `move` to move items from the head of a series to its tail. First, move one item, and then move a few items with `/part`.

12. Given the series `names: ["John" "Dave" "Jane" "Bob" "Sue"]`, write a code snippet that loops through the series and prints out the names that contain the character `a`. Then look for both the letters `a` and `e`.

Using Functions and Objects

6

This chapter is about modularizing code through the use of functions and objects.

We have already encountered a lot of built-in functions, such as `print` and `cd`, but of course you can write user-defined functions as well. When a program's code gets longer and more complex, you want to be able to give a name to certain code segments. For example, when processing a data stream from a file or the network, you'll want to have a `process-request` or `process-record` function that contains the logic of dealing with one chunk of data. That way, you can call this function each time you need it. This leads to less code that is better structured and more readable. Less code means fewer bugs! Functions can take parameters, local variables, and refinements, and we'll be exploring how to use these later on in the chapter.

Another way to group code is to define an object. Red is not class-based, like most object-oriented languages in common use today, such as Java, Python, C#, or Ruby, it takes a more prototype-based approach, where new objects can be created on the basis of an already existing object—its prototype. In this chapter, we will explore what you can do with objects in Red in depth.

In this chapter, we will cover the following topics:

- A fauna of functions
- Function attributes
- Working with functions
- Code is data and data is code
- Using objects

Technical requirements

You'll find the code for this chapter at `https://github.com/PacktPublishing/Learn-Red-Fundamentals-of-Red/tree/master/Chapter06`. If you have installed Red as indicated in `Chapter 2`, *Setting Up for Development*, you are good to go. You can work on Windows, OS X, or Linux. You can type or paste any code in the Red console to see its results, or you can use an editor, such as Visual Studio Code.

A fauna of functions

Red's built-in functions can be categorized as follows. The type is indicated within `()`:

- *operators* (`op!`), which can be used with infix notation, such as a + b, a / b, and so on.
- *native* (`native!`) functions, such as `if`, `either`, `while`, `throw`, `all`, `wait`, and so on; you can see a complete list by using `? op!` in the console.
- *routine* (`routine!`) functions, such as `exists?`, `write-clipboard`, and so on; you can see a list using `? routine!` It is also used in Red to define a function that calls a Red/System function (see `Chapter 10`, *Advanced Red*).

- *action* (`action!`) functions, such as `copy`, `move`, `clear`, `to`, `form`, and so on; you can see a complete list using `? action!`

  The native, routine, and action functions are *written in Red/System*. Action functions are special in that they are *polymorphic*—they are defined for more than one datatype. Which action code is executed depends on the type of its first argument.

- *mezzanine* (`function!`) functions, which are higher-level functions *written in Red*; you can see a complete list using `? function!`

In this section, we'll cover the variety of ways that exist to define your own functions.

The do word

We will start by giving a name (a label) to a code block so that you can call that code by its name and evaluate it with the `do` word, which we already saw in action in the *Evaluation with do and reduce* section in `Chapter 3`, *Using Words, Values, and Types*. Here, the word `pri5` is bound to a piece of code, which prints five digits separated by dashes:

```
;-- see Chapter06/do-does-has-func.red:
pri5: [ repeat i 5 [prin i prin "-"] ]
do pri5 ;== 1-2-3-4-5- ; evaluate code block with label pri5
type? pri5 ;== block!
```

However, `pri5` is not yet a real function; it is still a block, and you have to invoke it with `do`.

The block could also contain interactive code, such as that shown in the following example:

```
do [
    pass: ask "Enter Password: "
    either pass = "secret" [
        print "Welcome back."
    ][
        print "Incorrect password."
    ]
]
```

We could even ask the user to interactively enter code while the program is running, and then execute that code to obtain a simple form of metaprogramming, as shown in the following code:

```
do [
    code: ask "Enter some code: "
    do append {print "Here's your running code..."} code
]
```

This could give us an output such as the following:

```
Enter some code:
 loop 3 [prin "Hi!"] ;<-- input from user to ask
 Here's your running code...
 Hi!Hi!Hi!
```

Building further on this example, we can make a very primitive REPL with one line of code:

```
;-- see Chapter06/processor.red:
; #include %../../../red-source/environment/console/CLI/input.red
forever [print do ask "=> "]
```

Here is a possible user interaction:

```
PS E:\Red\The_book_of_Red\code\ch6> ./processor
=> print "Hello from Red!"
Hello from Red!

=> loop 5 [prin "Hi"]
HiHiHiHiHi
=>
```

If you compile, remember to uncomment the `#include` line and adapt the path to `input.red` on your machine. This starts to show what is possible with metaprogramming in Red!

Of course, any errors in the code entered interactively will only become apparent when the program runs.

=> Now answer question 1 from the *Questions* section.

The does word

The simplest way to make your own function in Red is with the `does` word. Consider the following code:

```
;-- see Chapter06/do-does-has-func.red:
cls: does [ loop 100 [print newline] ] ; == func [][loop 100 [print
newline]]
cls ; call function cls
```

The `newline` phrase is the character that prints a new line.

In the preceding example, we create a function called `cls` that clears the output screen by printing 100 blank lines when it is called as `cls`. It is a function (`func`), as we can see from the return value when defining `cls`. You use `does` when you need a function that has no arguments and no local variables.

=> Now answer question 2 from the *Questions* section.

An important distinction should be made between the following two kinds of variables:

- Local variables, which are only known in the function body itself
- Global variables, which are known in the function as well as outside of it

The has word

To define a simple function that has no arguments but does have local variables that are defined in a block that comes before the code block, use `has` as follows:

```
calc-hours-year: has [number] [
    number: 365 * 24 ; number is local
    print number
]   ;== func [/local number][...]
calc-hours-year ;== 8760
number    ; *** Script Error: number has no value
```

The return value of `calc-hours-year` shows that it is a function (`func`) with a local `number` variable that is not known outside of the function. Another way to look at it is that `has` turned the words in its first block into local variables.

=> Now answer question 3 from the *Questions* section.

The func word

To define a function with argument(s), use the `func` word, as shown in the following function that performs an increment:

```
inc: func [n][n + 1] ;== func [n][n + 1]
inc   ; *** Script Error: inc is missing its n argument
inc 7 ;== 8
```

Note that a `func` needs its argument to be passed as a parameter by the calling code; otherwise, you get the error `... is missing its ... argument`. But, unlike most other programming languages, you don't have to enclose the parameters in parentheses `()` when you call the function.

By the way, you'll better understand the `:` or `get` word with a function example. The `inc` word (or better `inc n`) calls (evaluates) the function, but `:` returns its own value:

```
:inc          ;== func [n][n + 1]
get 'inc      ;== func [n][n + 1]
```

The following `func` sums its two arguments `a` and `b`:

```
sum: func [a b][
    number: a + b
    print number ; global variable
]                    ;== func [a b][...]
sum 3 5 ;== 8
print number + 1     ;== 9  ; number is a global variable
a                    ; *** Script Error: a has no value
```

It is important to remember that, in Red, a function must always be defined before it is used; otherwise, you get a `*** Script error: fname has no value` when calling the `fname` function. Always define your functions at the start of the program and call them later. However, the order in which the functions are defined doesn't matter; inside another function, a function can be called before it is defined.

Note that all variables defined in a `func` (such as `number` in the example) are *global*: They are known outside the function. If the variable already existed outside the function, its value would be changed by the function; we say that it is shadowing the global variable (try that out). This almost certainly leads to bugs. To avoid that conflict, you can define the `number` variable in the function as local, as shown here in the `sum` function:

```
number: 108                       ; global
sum: func [a b /local number][
    number: a + b
    print number                  ; local
]                                 ;== func [a b][...]
sum 3 5                           ;== 8
print number + 1                  ;== 109 ; global
```

Probably the best solution is to give it another name altogether.

The function word

The `function` word allows for the most complete function definition. We'll describe and show examples of all possible attributes in the next section. One key difference between it and the other forms is that `function` automatically makes its variables local, so `/local` is not necessary. Omitting `/local` from the previous example gives us `function sum`:

```
number: 108              ; global
sum: function [a b][
    number: a + b        ; local
```

```
    print number           ; local
]                          ;== func [a b /local number][...]
sum 3 5                    ;== 8
print number + 1           ;== 109 ; global
```

From the return value after the definition of sum, we can see that number is automatically made local—no conflict can occur between global and local values anymore.

If you really need to, you can force a variable to be global with /extern. Applying this would change our sum function to sum: function [a b /extern number][...], and number + 1 would now have the value 9.

The following table will help you to understand the different kinds of functions clearly:

What does it do?	does	has	func	function
Specify arguments	N	N	Y	Y
Specify local variables	N	Y	With /local	Default
Reference global variables	Y	Y	Default	With /extern

Everything in a function body is local, and everything in a func body is global. That's why it is better to use function in more complex code, because the code of a function is more isolated from the surrounding code.

=> Now answer question 4 from the *Questions* section.

Copying a local series

We mentioned this already in the *Copying a series* section in Chapter 5, *Working with Series and Blocks*, but as this is a pitfall for new Red programmers, we will stress it again here—a series (also called a **string**) local to a function should be initialized with a copy. If not, the series will keep its value over subsequent function calls, which is an unexpected result for newcomers. Here is a correct example of how to initialize a local series using a function:

```
correct: function[] [
    data: copy []            ; correct initialization!
    append data 108
    data
]

correct ;== [108]
correct ;== [108]
```

```
correct ;== [108]
```

Run the snippet with `data: []` to see for yourself!

Function attributes

In this section, we will learn about giving arguments a type, how to return values from a function, how to define refinements, how to document a function, and how to do error-handling with functions.

Passing arguments

Here, we must make a distinction between single, so called `scalar!` values, such as numbers, dates, chars, and so on (See *The type system* section in Chapter 3, *Using Words, Values, and Types*), and all other values:

- Scalar values are passed *by value*, which means that a copy of the value is sent to the function
- Other values are passed *by reference*, which means that a reference to the value is sent to the function

The consequence of this is that scalar values cannot be changed by a function, whereas other values (such as series and objects) are changed. This can be seen in the following code snippet:

```
;-- see Chapter06/function-attributes.red:
passing-ref: function [data][
    append data 108
]

data: [2 3 7 42]
passing-ref data

data    ;== [2 3 7 42 108]
```

Typing arguments

Previously, we saw an increment `inc: func [n][n + 1]` function. This function takes a n parameter, but no type is specified for n. inc works for numbers (`inc 3.14 returns 4.14`), but not, for example, for strings, because the + operation is not defined for strings.

So when we use `inc "abc"`, it shows the `*** Script Error: + does not allow string!` for its `value1` argument error.

This dynamic typing, which you perhaps know from Python, Ruby, or JavaScript, makes functions very flexible and general, but also vulnerable to these runtime errors.

In Red, typing is optional, which means you can work this way, but you can also indicate an argument's type as shown in the following screenshot:

```
inc: func [n [integer!]][n + 1]
```

Here we see you can restrict the type of the argument `n` to `integer!`. The reason could simply be that you don't need a general function. In this example, this forces the arguments to be of a certain datatype:

- `inc 3.14` gives the `*** Script Error: inc does not allow float!` for its `n` argument error
- `inc "abc"` returns the `*** Script Error: inc does not allow string!` for its `n` argument error

This tells us what is wrong with the function call when testing.

Developers who want to use your function now also see that an integer parameter is required here, so this is a form of implicit documentation.

Typing arguments also allows the compiler to produce much more efficient native code.

In our previous example, we could have typed the function as follows:

```
passing-ref: function [ data [block!] ] [ ... ]
```

You can specify multiple types, like the following example:

```
inc: func [n [integer! float!]][n + 1]
inc 3.14      ;== 4.14
```

You can also specify a supertype (`typeset!`) of these types:

```
inc: func [n [number!]][n + 1]
```

=> Now answer question 5 from the *Questions* section.

Return values – return and exit

When the code in a function has been executed, control returns to the line after the function was called and a value is returned. This value is simply the last value computed in the function, such as the value `n + 1` in the `inc` example.

If you want to return a value earlier, you can do so with the `return` word. Control then also returns to where the function was called. Look at the following example, which is a `search-val` function that searches for a value in a given series. It returns the match and the rest of the series when found with `return series`; if no match is found, the `none` value is returned as the last value of the function:

```
search-val: func [series value] [
    forall series [
        if (first series) = value [
            return series
        ]
    ]
    none
]

search-val [10 20 30 40] 30     ;== [30 40]
search-val [10 20 30 40] 9      ;== none
```

To return multiple values from a function, return a block that has been reduced, such as the one in the following version of `search-val`:

```
search-val: func [series value] [
    forall series [
        if (first series) = value [
            return reduce [series index? series]
        ]
    ]
    none
]

search-val [10 20 30 40] 30            ;== [[30 40] 3]
```

You can also indicate that the return value must be of a certain type, as shown in the following example where we affirm that the `double` function returns an `integer` value:

```
double: function [
    n [integer!]
    return: [integer!]
][
    2 * n
]
```

If you want to leave a function without returning a value, use the `exit` word.

For readability, it is better that the contents of the first block get split on to several lines when indicating the types. This becomes even more natural when adding refinements and documentation strings.

Refinements

User-defined functions can also have refinements, which are like switches that can be optionally specified when calling a function. In the following example, we define a `sum` function with a `/avg` refinement:

```
sum: func [arg1 arg2 /avg][
    either avg [arg1 + arg2 / 2][arg1 + arg2]
]
sum 3 5        ;== 8
sum/avg 3 5    ;== 4
```

A refinement is tested as a Boolean value with the same name, but without the `/`. Also, don't leave a space between the function name and the refinement when calling `sum/avg`.

A refinement can also have a value, as shown in the following example:

```
div-sum: func [arg1 arg2 /div n][
    either div [arg1 + arg2 / n][arg1 + arg2]
]

div-sum 3 5              ;== 8
div-sum/div 3 5 4        ;== 2
```

Note that the refinement value follows the parameters. Better not overuse this, because it affects readability.

=> Now answer questions 6 and 7 from the *Questions* section.

Code style and documentation strings

When a function starts to get more complex, incorporating arguments, refinements, return values, and so on, its code must stay readable, following a standard layout. Also, when used in production, functions and all their parts should have documentation. We can provide this with `docstrings`.

Here is how a general function should be styled:

```
func-name: func [
        "Comments for the function itself"
        arg1    [type1!] "Describe 1st argument"
        arg2    [type2!] "Describe 2nd argument"
        /ref1           "Describe refinement"
                argref1 [type1]
        return: [type3!] "Describe return value"
][
    ; function body
]
```

Here is a fully documented function in the standard layout:

```
max: function [
        "Return the maximum of 2 numbers"
        arg1 [number!] "First number argument"
        arg2 [number!] "Second number argument"
][
        either arg1 > arg2 [
            arg1
        ][
            arg2
        ]
]
max 42 7    ;== 42
```

When you ask `help max` or simply `? max`, these documentation comments are shown in the REPL:

```
>> help max
USAGE:
MAX arg1 arg2

DESCRIPTION:
Return the maximum of 2 numbers.
MAX is a function! value.

ARGUMENTS:
arg1 [number!] "First number argument".
arg2 [number!] "Second number argument".
```

Working with functions

In this section, we will talk about how to make functions resistant to possible errors.

Error handling

In the previous section, we saw that passing the wrong type of argument to a function causes the program to terminate with an error message. Is there a way to guard functions against wrong types and still let the program continue? We know how to test types with `type?`, so we can do that instead. Here is a version of the `inc` function that is untyped, but protected against the possibility of n not being an integer:

```
inc: func [n] [
    if not integer? n [
        print ["n must be an integer, not a" (type? n)]
        exit
    ]
    n + 1
]

inc 9       ; == 10
inc pi      ; == n must be an integer, not a float
inc "abc"   ; == n must be an integer, not a string
```

Instead of the `if not type? n` test, we can also make this somewhat more readable:

```
inc: func [n][
    unless integer? n [
        print ["n must be an integer, not a " (type? n)]
        exit
    ]
    n + 1
]
```

This way, we can protect the start of a function with a number of tests, ensuring that, when the main logic starts, the input is reliable:

```
guarded-func: function [arguments][
    unless condA [ print "error-message" exit]
    unless condB [ print "error-message" exit]
    ; main logic
]
```

Red has some handy functions available to do this kind of protective test. The following are some examples:

- `zero?` returns `true` if the value is zero (0, 0.0, #"0", 0x0).
- `none?` returns `true` if the value is `none`.
- `positive?` and `negative?` return `true` if the number value is > than 0 or < than 0.
- `integer?`, `float?`, and `number?` are used to test the type of a number. In fact, this type of test is available for all types and built-in typesets!

Using these, we could simplify our previous guard statements to `if not integer? n` or `unless integer? n`.

Only if the guard cannot be expressed as an `if` test should you test dangerous code with `if error? try`.

Applying this to our `inc` example, this would become the following:

```
inc: func [n /local result][
    if error? try [result: n + 1][
        print ["n must be an integer, not a " (type? n)]
        exit
    ]
    result
]
```

```
inc 9        ;== 10
inc "Red"    ;n must be an integer, not a string
```

Another way to go about this is to let the function generate errors under certain conditions, but only catch the error when the function is called. For instance, here is an average function that goes wrong when count is 0:

```
average: function [
    total [number!] count [integer!]] [
    if zero? count [
        cause-error 'math 'zero-divide []
    ]
    total / count ; might cause an error
]

average 354 6    ;== 59
average 354 0    ;*** Math Error: attempt to divide by zero
```

We can call this function with error? try and print out either the result or the error message, as follows:

```
either error? result: try [average 354 0] [
    print ["Error id: " result/id]
][
    print ["No error, the result is: " result]
]
;== Error id: zero-divide
```

This is overkill for this simple example, but it could be useful in certain circumstances. Instead of causing an error and catching it outside the function, it is often easier to simply test the error condition, report it, and then continue with the program after the function, as follows:

```
average: function [
    total [number!] count [integer!]] [
    if zero? count [return "Divide by zero"]
    total / count ; might cause an error
]

average 354 0 ;== "Divide by zero"
```

If you simply want to leave the function without any message, simply use exit:

```
if zero? count [exit]
```

=> Now answer question 8 from the *Questions* section.

Recursive functions

A function is recursive when it calls itself with another value for its argument. After a number of recursive calls, a base case must be reached that ends the recursion (otherwise it will go on indefinitely). A common example is the calculation of the factorial of a number, which goes like this:

4! = 4 x 3 x 2 x 1 = 4 x 3! = 4 x 3 x 2! = 4 x 3 x 2 x 1! = 4 x 3 x 2 x 1 x 0! = 24 with the base case—0! = 1.

This can be easily translated into a Red `fact` function:

```
fact: func [n] [
        if n = 0 [ return 1]
        n * fact n - 1
]

fact 4 ; 24
```

Here we used `func`, but, sometimes, recursion may need local variables, and `function` will then be more useful, because, for a `function`, locals are the default.

Now evaluate the following:

```
fact 4.0     ; (1) == 24.0
fact -4      ; (2) == *** Internal Error: stack overflow
fact "abc"   ; (3) *** Script Error: - does not allow string! for its value1
argument
fact 21      ; (4) *** Math Error: math or number overflow
```

So you can see that a lot can be done to make this function more safe! Let's look at some useful rules for doing this:

- The argument should be an integer
- The argument cannot be negative
- The argument cannot be a string
- Because `fact 21` is too big for an integer, calculation should stop at `fact 20`

It is left to you as an exercise (question 9 in the *Questions* section) to document this function and implement the guard tests.

Importing functions with do

Soon after starting a project, you will start getting a lot of functions, and you may ask, *where should I put their code?* You will likely want to have a compact `main.red` file, which starts your program and can call functions stored in other files.

Let's say one of these files is called `useful-functions.red`, and contains the functions `fact` from the previous section and the `check` function:

```
;-- see Chapter06/useful-functions.red:
check: func [list] [
    answer: "safe"
    foreach l list [
        if find l "--" [answer: "unsafe"]
    ]
    answer
]
```

 What it does is not that important here. It goes through a `list` of names, and returns the `safe` string, but if any name in the list contains `--`, `check` returns the `unsafe` string.

This is depicted with the following example:

```
names1: ["Joe" "Dan" "Sh--" "Bill"]
names2: ["Paul" "Tom" "Mike" "John"]
check names1 ;==  unsafe
check names2 ;==  safe
```

How can we call `check` from within `main.red`?

If `main.red` doesn't contain any reference to `check`, we obviously get a `Script Error: check has no value`.

Perhaps your first idea is to use `#include %useful-functions.red`, as we saw in our guessing game in `Chapter 4`, *Code-Controlling Structures*. This inclusion of functions works; the code in `main.red` now executes correctly:

```
print append "names1 is " check names1
print append "names2 is " check names2
```

We will get the following output:

```
names1 is unsafe
names2 is safe
```

Our versatile `do` word also does the trick with `do %useful-functions.red` at the start of `main.red`. Note that `do` used this way only works with interpretation, and not when the script is compiled. These are the two ways to import a Red script in your code.

Code is data and data is code

Now we come back to the powerful introspective and metaprogramming features of Red—namely, how Red can work with code in the same way as data.

Using reflection on functions

Functions are first-class objects in Red. You can give your own functions, or even built-in ones, another name, as shown here:

```
;-- see Chapter06/reflection-functions.red:
pr: :print                ;== make native! [[
pr ["Hello" "Red"]    ;== Hello Red
```

The `:` prevents the function from executing; `pr: get 'print` does the same thing.

This shows Red's flexibility and power; not only changing the name, but even changing the meaning of built-in words is possible. As always, with great power comes great responsibility. Use these and the other metaprogramming features to come sparely, and above all, wisely!

Functions can contain other functions that are local to that function and that can access all its variables.

A function can also return a function as a result, as shown in the following code example:

```
make-timer: func [code] [
    func [time] code
]

timer: make-timer [wait time]
timer 3 ;== none
```

The `code` variable gets a `wait time` value, and the `time` variable gets the a `3` value.

The source word

You can look at the Red source code of user-defined and mezzanine functions with the `source` word.

For example, typing `source replace` in the REPL shows you the source code of the `replace` function we encountered in the previous chapter. Here is the output of this command:

```
replace: func [
        series [series!]
        pattern
        value
        /all
    ...
    ]
```

It's only about 30 lines, but we have shown only the beginning here; type in the command in the console to see the entire output.

This also works for your own functions—for example, type `source fact` after you have defined `fact` in the REPL or in a code file, and you can see its code! You can even use `source source`.

> You can learn a lot from viewing this code; maybe you can use portions of it for your own functions or new versions of existing functions.

The body-of function

The `body-of` function, as its name suggests, returns the body of a defined function. For example, when used with our `check` function from the previous section, we get `body-of :check`, which returns the following:

```
[
    answer: "safe"
    foreach l list [
            if find l "--" [answer: "unsafe"]
    ]
    answer
]
```

It also works for built-in functions, such as `body-of :replace`.

Perhaps this doesn't seem so useful at first. But think about this—the body of a function is only a series of code lines. This series of lines can be manipulated with all of the words defined for `series!`, like it is data. This opens up lots of new possibilities!

Changing the header and body of a function through code

Just to hint at to how flexible Red really is, consider this `fp1` function:

```
fp1: function [x [integer!] y [string!]] [
    prin [x "- "]
    print y
]
```

Let's name the header (this is the part where the parameters are declared) and the body:

```
header: [x [integer!] y [string!]]
body: [
    prin [x "- "]
    print y
]
```

We can now rewrite our function as `fp1-alt: function header body`.

The `body` phrase has to be on the same line as `function` and `header`; otherwise, you get the `Script Error: function is missing its body argument` error (only in the Red console).

Both functions still work the same, as shown in the following code fragment:

```
fp1 108 "Red"       ;== 108 - Red
fp1-alt 108 "Red"   ;== 108 - Red
```

Now let's manipulate `body` to reverse the second argument in the output:

```
fp2: function header replace copy body 'y [reverse y]
fp2 109 "Red"     ;== 109 - deR
```

Note that you need to treat `y` as a literal word, `'y`; otherwise, you get the `Script Error: y has no value` error.

Here is another example, where we construct the parameters and body part of the function:

```
params: []
body: []
append params load {message}
append body load {print message}
prn: function params body    ;-- function definition
prn "Hello World"            ;== Hello World
source prn                   ;== prn: func [message][print message]
```

Again, the message must be enclosed as a string here with { }, in order to prevent evaluation. We can also use the literal ' word notation, replacing the two `append` statements with the following:

```
append params 'message
append body [print message]
```

This produces exactly the same result.

Code is just data – load

Lines of code in Red are just data structures. Let's start with some very basic code, such as an arithmetic expression—for example, `3.14 ** 2` , calculating the square of 3.14, which is 9.8596. You write your code in an editor, so it's basically a string, right?

```
;-- see Chapter06/code-data.red:
calc: "3.14 ** 2"
type? calc     ;== string!
calc           ;== "3.14 ** 2"
```

Here, `:calc` or `get 'calc` return the same result as `calc`.

Now we must transform this string expression into something Red can work with—namely, a series in a block. This can be done with the `load` word, which loads the string into memory, parses it, and turns it into Red values:

```
code: load calc   ;== [3.14 ** 2]
code              ;== [3.14 ** 2]
type? code        ;== block!
length? code      ;== 3    ; code is only a series at this point
```

Using the `code` word doesn't do anything yet. Our `do` word comes to the rescue:

```
do code    ;== 9.8596
```

So we need `load` to turn the expression into data that Red can understand, and, because data is code, `do` can run that data.

Now let's manipulate our `code`, which is, after all, just data. Let's replace `3.14` with `pi` and calculate the third power of it:

```
code/1: pi          ;== 3.141592653589793
code/3: 3           ;== 3
code                ;== [3.141592653589793 ** 3]
do code             ;== 31.00627668029982
```

Changing the operator is just as easy, but we have to use the literal ' syntax here so that – does not evaluate, as follows:

```
code/2: -        ;*** Script Error: - operator is missing an argument
; solution:
code/2: '-          ;== -
code                ;== [3.141592653589793 - 3]
do code             ;== 0.1415926535897931
```

The type of – is just `word!`; you have to use `get` to get its value, an operation, `op!`.

We can see this using the `/2` notation or by using `second`:

```
code/2                   ;== -
second code              ;== -
type? code/2             ;== word!
type? second code        ;== word!
:code/2                  ;== -
type? get second code    ;== op!
```

We can expand the `code` expression as we like, for example, refer to the following code:

```
append code [- pi]       ;== [3.141592653589793 - 3 - pi]
code                     ;== [3.141592653589793 - 3 - pi]
do code                  ;== -3.0
```

It will now be clear that, until you evaluate the code (with `do`), it's just data.

In the same way that we renamed `print` as `pr` in the preceding code, we could even change the – word to mean the + operation:

```
-: :+            ;== make op! [[ "Returns the sum of the two values" ...
code             ;== [3.141592653589793 - 3 - pi]
do code          ;== 9.283185307179586
```

The expression still looks the same, but it now has a completely different meaning! Of course, you shouldn't be doing this with built-in words; this is just to show the reflective power of Red.

Now let's explore our `inc` function in the same way, using `inc: func [n][n + 1]`:

```
fun: "inc: func [n][n + 1]"      ;== "inc: func [n][n + 1]"
type? fun                        ;== string!
code: load fun                   ;== [inc: func [n] [n + 1]]
code                             ;== [inc: func [n] [n + 1]]
type? code                       ;== block!
```

At this stage, `code` is still a `block!`, `inc 7` returns a `*** Script Error: inc has no value` error, and `load` doesn't run anything. We need `do` to turn that data into a function:

```
do code        ;== func [n][n + 1]
inc 7          ;== 8
type? :inc     ;== function!
```

The `code` block, which has the `[inc: func [n] [n + 1]]` value, needs to be evaluated in order for the `function!` value to be constructed in memory, which is what `do` does.

Let's examine the type of each item of `code` with `foreach item code [print [type? item mold item]]`.

This prints the following output:

```
set-word inc:
word func
block [n]
block [n + 1]
```

As you may notice, our `code` block holds four values of the `set-word!` and `word!` types and two `block!` entities. Every value in Red has its datatype!

> To summarize, all code in Red is also data, so code can be very easily manipulated at any stage of execution. In another sense, data becomes code when we instruct Red to interpret it.

Other dynamic languages, such as JavaScript and Ruby, have a similar `eval` keyword, but `eval` immediately runs the source code string; the string is not loaded and turned into data, as it is with Red.

This code-as-data philosophy makes serialization and persistence of code very easy; sending code remotely or saving snapshots of code from a running program to disk are one-liners in Red, as we will see in the next chapter. This could also be applied for features such as code hot-swapping and live debugging of a running program.

Using objects

Now we will discover how Red works with objects, which is probably different from what you are used to in classical object-oriented languages, such as Java, C#, Python, and Ruby. But first, we meet the make word.

The make word

In the *Using error?* section in Chapter 4, *Code-Controlling Structures,* we used probe to get more details of a specific error, and this returned an output starting with **make** error! [...]. The error! is effectively an object that was constructed with make.

It turns out that make can be used to construct a new value for any datatype. It needs the type and, as a second argument, a specification for that type. This can be a value or a memory allocation, or another specification in the case of datatype!, native!, action!, routine!, and event!.

Here are some examples:

```
;-- see Chapter06/objects.red:
i: make integer! 5              ; == 5     ; (1)
output: make string! 1000       ; == ""    ; (2)
blk: make block! 20             ; == []    ; (3)
```

In line (1), the specification is the integer itself, in line (2), the number of characters in the string, and in line (3), the initial size of the block.

The make word is useful when you know your code will need a value of a certain type and size, but you also initially don't know its content. In such a case, it is better for performance purposes to construct a series dynamically with make, instead of using a literal such as copy "".

Working with objects

In languages, such as Java or Ruby, you first create a class with attributes and methods, like a kind of template, and then you can create objects from that class, often by using a `new` constructor, like

```
new ClassName(...).
```

Red doesn't know classes. Instead, it only uses objects, which contain data (attributes or fields) and/or functions (methods). You create objects either by cloning existing objects or starting from the base `object!` value. This is why Red has a prototype-based object model (instead of a class-based one)—objects are made by reusing existing objects. This model has the advantage of being simple and efficient. Other languages that work the same way for objects are JavaScript and Lua.

The Red system also has internal objects. An important example is the `system` object we explored in `Chapter 3`, *Using Words, Values, and Types*.

Creating objects

The first way to create an object is to use `make` on the base `object!` datatype. Let's create a `square1` object with a `length` value and a `display` function, as follows:

```
square1: make object! [
    length: 10
    display: does [ print ["Length of square1 is" length] ]
]   ;== make object! [ ... ]
```

Secondly, instead of `make object!`, you can use the shorter `object` or `context`.

To check whether a word refers to an object, use `object?`:

```
object? square1     ;== true
ser: [2 7 42 108]
object? ser         ;== false
```

Working with fields and functions

Accessing a variable or a function within an object is done using the / (path) notation, which we already encountered as the way to access the elements of a series by index, or using the file-path notation:

```
square1/length     ;== 10
square1/display    ; Length of square1 is 10
```

This works the same as the . (dot) notation using the
square1.length and square1.display() classes in other languages.

In the same way, you can change data in the object:

```
square1/length: 5    ;== 5
square1/length       ;== 5
```

Another way to do this uses get in or set in to access a field using the literal
' word notation:

```
get in square1 'length      ;== 10
set in square1 'length 5     ;== 5
```

The set word can also be used to initialize all fields to none, or to give one or more fields a new value:

```
set square1 none        ;== none
square1                 ;== make object! [length: none display: none]
set square1 [3 "Red"]   ;== [3 "Red"]
square1                 ;== make object! [length: 3 display: "Red"]
```

An object can contain executable code outside of its functions. This code is executed when constructing the object, and only then:

```
square1: make object! [
    print "Entering square1"
    length: 10
    display: does [ print ["Length of square1 is" length] ]
]    ;== make object! [ ... ]
; output:
; Entering square1 ;== make object! [ ... ]

square1/length      ;== 10
```

If the value of a field is not known during object creation, simply give it a value of none:

```
person: object [
    name: none
    show: does [print name]
]   ;== make object! [ ... ]

person/name: "Johnson"
person/show ;== "Johnson"
```

An object can refer to itself in its own code with self:

```
creature: object [
    name: "Amygdala"
    show: does [print self]
]   ;== make object! [ ... ]

creature/show
; name: "Amygdala"
; show: func [][print self]
```

This is analogous to self or this in other languages.

Objects can be nested—that is, an object can contain other objects. For example, a person object could contain an address field, which in turn could contain street, city, state, and postal-code fields:

```
person1: object [
    name: "Mueller"
    tel: none
    address: object [
        street: "Kensington Street 28"
        postal-code: 86512
        city: "Burmington"
        state: "OH"
    ]
]

person1/address/state    ;== "OH"
```

Nested fields are accessed with a composite / notation.

Copying objects and inheritance

Let's start with a really simple person object—`person1: object [ name: "Mueller" tel: ""]`.

The following code applies what we have learned in the *Assigning and copying* section in `Chapter 3`, *Using Words, Values, and Types*—namely, `""`:

```
person1: object [ name: "Mueller" tel: none ]
person2: person1
person1/tel: "108-4271"
person2/tel  ;== "108-4271"
person3: copy person1
person3 ;== make object! [ name: "Mueller" tel: "108-4271"]
person1/tel: "333-4271"
person3 ;== make object! [ name: "Mueller" tel: "108-4271"]
```

The `person2` word references the same object as `person1`, so it changes whenever `person1` changes. The `person3` word is a *new object*, with all values copied from `person1` (a clone), and so it is independent from `person1`, but it also consumes additional memory.

In object-oriented languages, you can make a class inherit all its properties and methods from a superclass, and add some new ones of its own. This can be done very easily in Red—Use `make` with the starting object, and add new properties and/or methods. This is shown as follows:

```
person4: make person1 [id-number: #MFG-932-741-A]
person4
;== make object! [name: "Mueller" tel: "333-4271" id-number: #MFG-932-741-
A]
person4/name: "Johnson"
person1 ;== make object! [name: "Mueller" tel: "333-4271"]
```

The `person4` object is a new object, which has inherited the contents of `person1`, but can change independently. You could also change field values while creating the new object, which is shown as follows:

```
person4: make person1 [name: "Johnson" id-number: #MFG-932-741-A]
```

Now we understand that a `copy` of a `person1` object can also be written as `make person1 []`.

=> Now answer question 10 from the *Questions* section.

This mechanism can also be used to merge two or more objects, a kind of multiple inheritance:

```
a: object [x: 5]
b: object [y: 10]
c: make a b               ;== make object! [x: 5 y: 10]
d: object [x: 3 y: 10]
c: make a d               ;== make object! [x: 3 y: 10]
```

If the starting objects contain the same field(s), the last object takes priority.

Through copying and inheriting, it is easy to create a lot of objects. Objects are datatypes that consume memory, a lot of memory if the objects are big and you keep many of them around. In such a case, it is better to keep cloning objects at a minimum, and instead work with references to objects. Also, give objects you don't need anymore the none value.

So you see, creating objects from existing objects is very flexible!

In the current release (0.6.3), Red has no **garbage collector** (**GC**) to clean up and regain unused memory. That may limit long-running programs, or ones that do a lot of data manipulation. A simple version of a GC will be available in Version 0.6.4, while a full version will integrate with the normal master branch in Version 0.8.5.

Looking inside an object

Sometimes, you need to find out whether a certain object has a certain field (or function). The find phrase returns true if the field exists, none if it doesn't:

```
find person1 'tel          ;== true
find person1 'id-number    ;== none
```

Again, you have to use the ' literal word syntax. Once you know the field exists, access its value with the familiar path notation, such as person1/tel   ;== "333-4271". However, you could also use select with the same notation:

```
select person1 'tel         ;== "333-4271"
select person1 'id-number    ;== none
```

Some reflective words exist to get the contents, the list of fields, or the list of the values of an object, as shown in the following snippet:

```
person1: object [ name: "Mueller" tel: "333-4271" ]
body-of person1      ;== [name: "Mueller" tel: "333-4271"]
words-of person1     ;== [name tel]
values-of person1    ;== ["Mueller" "333-4271"]
```

A powerful `on-change*` function can be defined inside an object, which detects when a field in an object is changed (with the / syntax). The changed field is contained in `word`; `old` and `new` contain the former and the changed value. Here is an example that shows that a person's name has been changed:

```
person1: object [
    name: "Mueller" tel: "333-4271"
    on-change*: func [word old new /local msg] [
        if word = 'name [
            msg: "The person's name is changed!"
            print ["Warning:" msg]
        ]
    ]
]

person1/name: "Johnson" ;== Warning: The person's name is changed!
```

=> Now answer question 11 from the *Questions* section.

Summary

Now you can use functions to make code more succinct and readable. We explored the different function forms that exist (`does`, `has`, `func`, and `function`), and the awesome power of `do` for evaluating and importing code. We learned to declare function arguments, refinements, and return values, giving them a type when appropriate. Functions should be documented, and we saw how to do this. We also explored some important techniques for performing error handling and writing recursive functions. Finally, we demonstrated how code in Red can be treated as data, making metaprogramming possible.

We also learned how to make objects with fields and methods, as well as how to make new objects from existing objects and how to explore the contents of an object.

In the next chapter, you'll learn how to read and store data in files, making a whole lot of new applications possible.

Questions

1. Run the following code, both interpreted and compiled.

```
mycode: [prnt "Hello" halt]
do mycode
```

Explain the results.

2. Rewrite the first `do` example in this chapter with `does`.

3. What is the difference between the `has1` and `has2` functions in the following code?

```
has1: has [][
    num: 108 - 42
    print num
]

has2: has [num][
    num: 108 - 42
    print num
]
```

4. What are the values of `num1` and `num2` after executing the following code? Explain.

```
ex-glob: function [
    /extern num1 ]
[
    num1: 13
    num2: 42
]

num1: 100 ;== 100
num2: 200 ;== 200
ex-glob
```

5. Define a `sum` function that sums two numbers, n and m. Use argument typing.

6. Write a `testref` function that takes two number parameters. The function should have a `/add` refinement that returns their sum, and a `/sub` refinement that returns their subtraction.

7. Write an `average` function that takes a series of numbers and returns its average.

8. Red has a built-in `sqrt` function to calculate the square root of a number. For a negative argument, the mathematical result is a complex number. In Red, this function returns `NaN` (Not a Number): `sqrt -4   ;== 1.#NaN`. Write your own `mysqrt` function that uses `sqrt`, but guards against a negative input argument with `unless`. Also make sure that the input is a number! Test all kinds of input.

9. Fully implement all guards for the `fact` function mentioned in the section on recursive functions.

10. Make a `car` object that contains fields such as brand, selling price, VAT (or discount) percentage, and number of cars in stock. The object should also contain a function that calculates the total price with VAT included, and a function that calculates the total stock value. Make a more concrete object, such as, for example `bmw` or `tesla`, and test the object by calling the functions.

11. Adapt the `on-change` function in `person1` so that the name value cannot be changed.

Working with Files 7

Red is very well equipped to work with and manipulate files and folders easily.

As early as `Chapter 3`, *Using Words, Values, and Types*, we saw our first examples of the `file!` type, with its `%` and `/` syntax. From the type hierarchy, we can observe that `file!` is a subtype of `string!`, and, from there, a subtype of `series!`, and so all the functions we have seen for series also apply to files.

We'll encounter such examples in this chapter. But, above all, we will learn how to use files as data stores. We will examine reading and writing files, either data files, or code files. We'll develop our knowledge of the topic using an ongoing example. By the end of this chapter, you will know how to download stock quotes or other files from the internet and save them to local files.

We'll explore the following topics:

- Selecting a file or folder
- Working with paths and directories
- Reading and writing data files
- Loading and saving files
- Downloading currency exchange rates

Technical requirements

You'll find the code for this chapter at `https://github.com/PacktPublishing/Learn-Red-Fundamentals-of-Red/tree/master/Chapter07`. If you have installed Red as instructed in `Chapter 2`, *Setting Up for Development*, you are good to go. You can work on Windows, OS X, or Linux. For the bigger examples in this chapter, you can best use an editor such as Visual Studio Code.

Selecting a file or folder

In the *Getting input from the user* section in `Chapter 3`, *Using Words, Values, and Types*, we saw how to use `ask` to get user console input. Red also has special words that can be used to ask for a file or a folder.

Using `request-file` in the REPL or from a script pops up a dialog that prompts the user to select a file from the local file system:

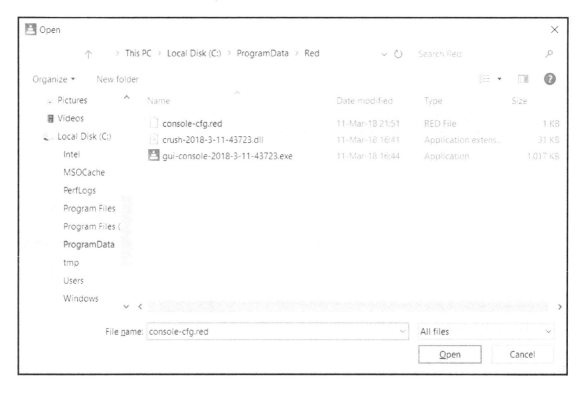

In this screen, you can navigate to the file you need. Pressing the **Open** button returns the file name with its complete path as a `file!` ; choosing **Cancel** returns `none`. The result from the script is as follows:

```
;-- see Chapter07/ask-file.red:
file: request-file
probe file          ;== %/E/Red/red.bat   ; this file was chosen in File
Explorer
```

In the same way, we have `request-dir`:

This gives us the following result when the **Program Files** map is chosen and the **OK** button pressed:

```
dir: request-dir
probe dir           ;== %/C/Program%20Files/
```

The `%20` character represents the space in the string `Program Files`.

These words come with some handy refinements:

- You can use `/title` to either change the pop-up window title (for `request-file`) or display text beneath the window title (for `request-dir`). For example, `request-file/title "Browse to the application:"`.
- You can use `/file` to fill in the name of the file that you want to browse for. For example, `request-file/file %"app1.exe"`.

- Analogously, `/dir` sets the starting directory—`request-dir/dir %"/C/Windows"`.
- Use `/save` if you want to write to a file in a save dialog window—`request-file/file/save %data1.txt`.
- To search for specific files, use `/filter`. For example, `request-file/filter ["data files" "*.dat" "executables" "*.exe"]`.
- You can even let the user select multiple files with `/multi`; their names are returned in a block. For example, `request-file/multi ;== [%/E/Red/red.bat %/E/Red/todo.txt]`.

Both these words can be used in nongraphical console apps or in graphical apps. Also, a `request-font` word exists to let the user choose a character font.

Working with file paths and directories

Red by default uses the forward slash, `/`, in some sort of universal path notation. The `/` character denotes the root of the current drive, `./` denotes the current folder, and `../` points to the folder one step up in the file hierarchy. As we have seen in the `guess-number.red` script from Chapter 4, *Code-Controlling Structures*, this `../` notation is used to denote a path relative to the current folder. An absolute path starts with a drive-letter or with the root drive `/`.

> Use relative paths instead of absolute paths to make your scripts machine-independent. Also make sure that your program can run on Windows as well as on Linux or OS X.

Converting a string to a file is done with `to-file`, but only the syntax changes, nothing else is checked.

If you need to transform a file path to a specific platform notation such as Windows, use the `to-local-file` function, such as in the following:

```
;-- see Chapter07/working-with-files-directories.red:
to-local-file %/E/Red/red.bat    ;== "E:\Red\red.bat"
```

Conversely, to convert a specific path notation to a platform-independent format, use `to-red-file`, as shown in the following code:

```
to-red-file "E:\Red\red.bat"    ;== %/E/Red/red.bat
```

Both of the preceding functions have a `/full` refinement to turn the file path into an absolute path if needed.

```
to-local-file/full %red.bat      ;== "E:\Red\red.bat"
```

Note that Red will automatically transform a platform-specific path with \ to a standard notation, if you enclose the path within "":

```
write %"C:\ProgramData\Red\test.txt" "test"
```

Here is a quick overview of some handy functions for your reference:

- Both `pwd` and `what-dir` return the current working folder, which at the start is the folder from which the current program is executed—for example, for the REPL—`pwd` `;== %/C/ProgramData/Red/`, `get-current-dir` returns the same value in string format—`"C:\ProgramData\Red"`.

- Both `cd` and `change-dir` change the current directory, and with it the values of the functions in the previous bullet—`cd %/E/test`, `;== %/E/test/`, and `pwd` `;== %/E/test/`.

- Each of the words `dir`, `ls`, and `list-dir folder` gives you the contents of the current or the given folder.

- The characters `file?` and `dir?` respectively test whether their argument is a file or a folder:

  ```
  file? %/E/Red/red.bat ;== true
  dir? %/E/Red/          ;== true (trailing / is needed)
  ```

- The phrase `make-dir` creates a new folder, with no error if this already exists:
  ```
  make-dir %scripts.
  ```

- To test whether a file or folder really exists, use `exists?`:

  ```
  exists? %/E/Red/red.bat      ;== true
  exists? %/E/Red/red2.bat     ;== false
  exists? %/E/NotExist/        ;== false
  ```

- The `suffix?` phrase returns the extension of a file—`suffix? %/E/Red/red.bat ;== %.bat`.

- The `size?` phrase returns a file's size in bytes, or `none` if it does not exist—size? %red.bat ;== 22.
- To delete a file, simply use `delete %file`. This returns `true` when it succeeds.

Reading and writing data files

The `read` and `write` words are good examples of the generalized way in which Red words work. They are used to read and write all sorts of files (text and binary data), but you can also use them with network ports or URLs (see the stock quotes example later in this chapter). If you have worked with files in other languages, you'll appreciate their ease of use; in Red, there is no need to open a file in a certain mode and close it afterwards!

Let's work with the exact same data from our `contacts` series example in Chapter 5, *Working with Series and Blocks*:

```
;-- see Chapter07/reading-and-writing-files.red:
contacts: [
    "John Smith" "123 Tomline Lane Forest Hills, NJ" "555-1234"
    "Paul Thompson" "234 Georgetown Pl. Grove, AL" "555-2345"
    "Jim Persee" "345 Pickles Pike Orange Grove, FL" "555-3456"
    "George Jones" "456 Topforge Court Mountain Creek, CO" ""
    "Tim Paulson" "" "555-5678"
]
```

Our first contact has the following data:

```
name: "John Smith"
address: "123 Tomline Lane Forest Hills, NJ"
phone: "555-1234"
```

Let's write this to a file called `contacts1`. The general syntax is `write %filename data`, where `data` can be of any type. However, each time you write to the same file, you overwrite the previous content. If we use `/append`, the data is appended to the end of the file:

```
write %contacts1 name
write/append %contacts1 address
write/append %contacts1 phone
```

The file is written in the folder that is given by `pwd`. If you need to store it in a different folder, use a complete file-path (relative or absolute) in the filename—for example, `%/E/Red/Tests/contacts1`. A suffix such as `.txt` is not needed, but you can add it if you want to.

If you open `contacts1` in an editor, you will see `John Smith123 Tomline Lane Forest Hills, NJ555-1234`. Reading this file with Red gives you the contents in one string:

```
read %contacts1    ;== {John Smith123 Tomline Lane Forest Hills, NJ555-1234}
```

If you try to read a file that does not exist, for example, `read %contacts99`, you will get an `*** Access Error: cannot open: %contacts99` error.

The different fields cannot be separated anymore. Let's write all data to one line, with each field separated by a semicolon (`;`) (we could have chosen whatever we wanted as a separator):

```
write %contacts1 rejoin [name ";" address ";" phone newline]
```

The `contacts1` file now contains `John Smith;123 Tomline Lane Forest Hills, NJ;555-1234`.

Now we want to store all our `contacts` data in a text file, `contacts2`, with one line per contact. We can do that by looping through the series, pattern matching the fields, and writing each contact on one line, as follows:

```
foreach [name address phone] contacts [
    write/append %contacts2 rejoin [name ";" address ";" phone newline]
]
```

To read this data back in, we could use `contents: read %contacts2`, but then the `contents` string contains the whole file. We would have to use `split` (see *Chapter 5, Working with Series and Blocks*) first on the newline character to separate our contacts, and then `split` on the `;` to get the separate fields of each contact.

But we can get each contact back as a separate string, all gathered in one block, with the following:

```
contents: read/lines %contacts2
```

This gives us the following result:

```
;== [{John Smith;123 Tomline Lane Forest Hills, NJ;555-1234} {Paul
Thompson;234 Georgetown Pl. Grove, AL;555-2345} {Jim Persee;345 Pickles
Pike Orange Grove, FL;555-3456} {George ...   ]
```

If you just want to write out the data block to a file, only one line is needed—namely, **write** `%contactsw contacts`—and the `contactsw` file then contains the following:

```
[
    "John Smith" "123 Tomline Lane Forest Hills, NJ" "555-1234"
    "Paul Thompson" "234 Georgetown Pl. Grove, AL" "555-2345"
    "Jim Persee" "345 Pickles Pike Orange Grove, FL" "555-3456"
    "George Jones" "456 Topforge Court Mountain Creek, CO" ""
    "Tim Paulson" "" "555-5678"
]
```

To write out each item in a series on a different line in a file, use `write/lines`, and use `write/lines/append` if you need to add content to an existing file. Try this out in question 1 in the *Questions* section. While you're at it, also do questions 2 and 3.

Use `read %.` to store all file and folder names in the current folder in a block with a return value such as `[%apps/ %articles/ %benchmarks/ %blockchain/ %books/ %build/ %cinfo %contactss ... ]`.

Working with binary files

If the file you work with contains only bytes (not readable text), as with multimedia files (pictures, audio, movies), add the `/binary` refinement, as shown in this example where a `png` image is loaded in a temporary variable `tmp` :

```
tmp: read/binary %red.png
```

```
;== #{
89504E470D0A1A0A0000000D49484452000002EE000002ED08060000007789E1
64000078C34944415478DAECDD079C645599F7F1E739F75655E7389DD3040686
0C8A202220028AB8200883AEBB20418220023A8489...}
```

Now we write `tmp` out to another file `red-copy.png`:

```
write/binary %red-copy.png tmp
```

To follow better Red's idiomatic way of writing, eliminate `tmp` and just write—`write/binary %red-copy2.png read/binary %red.png`.

The image! datatype

In fact, Red has a special `image!` datatype for picture files. Suppose we have a binary file with the Red logo image in it, named `logo.png`. Then we can read it into our program as follows:

```
img: load %logo.png
; == make image! [120x124 #{
; FFFFFFFFFFFFFFFFFFFFFFFFFFFFFFFFFFFFFFFF

img/size ;== 120x124
pick img 10 ;== 255.255.255.0                    (1)
poke img 10 150.125.100.0 ;== 150.125.100.0      (2)
```

We see that internally it is an `image!` object, and that the image data is of the `binary!` type. We can get the RGB (color) value of pixel `10`, as shown in line `(1)`, or even change it, as shown in line `(2)`. An `image!` is a `series!` type, so all actions applicable to series can be used on images.

Likewise, if you have the binary data, you can construct an image object in your code, like this:

```
img2: make image! [30x40 #{ ; binary image data...}]
```

Saving it to a `picture.png` file is just as easy with `write/binary %picture.png img2`.

A Faces Walkthrough Section, in `Chapter 9`, *Composing Visual Interfaces*, shows you how to show a picture file in an `image` face on a screen.

Downloading a file from the internet

Sometimes your app needs to get files from a website. Currently, `read` can do this for you using the HTTP protocol:

```
read http://www.red-lang.org/index.html
```

This gives the following string as return value:

```
;== {<!DOCTYPE html>^/<html class='v2' dir='ltr'
xmlns='http://www.w3.org/1999/xhtml'
xmlns:b='http://www.google.com/2005/gml/b'
xmlns:data='http://www.google.com/2005/gml/data' xml
```

This string can be captured in a data variable for further processing:

```
data: read http://www.red-lang.org/index.html
```

If you're only interested in a part of the web page, use `copy/part`:

```
data: copy/part read http://www.red-lang.org/index.html 15
; == "<!DOCTYPE html>"
```

You can also write it out to a local file, all in one line:

```
write %redhome.html read http://www.red-lang.org/index.html
```

In general, `read` and `write` are mostly used for reading and writing strings to storage media, but, as we showed in our examples, they can be used for binary files and block structures as well.

Release 0.7 will bring many more possibilities for data exchange through a network.

Loading and saving files

Red also has the `save` and `load` words, that can be used interchangeably with `write` and `read`. However, `save` and `load` are generally used to store more complex data structures, and in particular to store and load Red code. But we already know that in Red, code can be treated as data.

To see for yourself that `save` and `load` can be used for data, answer question 4 in the *Questions* section.

The `save` word can also be used to write data into a string or binary value.

In particular, if you have a file with data items separated by a space, `load` will transform that into a series with the items. Suppose we have a `names` file with the following contents:

```
"John" "Dave" "Jane" "Bob" "Sue" "Sarah" "Mikhail" "Rudolf" "Nenad"
```

If we use `load` to read in that file, we get the following:

```
;-- see Chapter07/saving-and-loading.red:
names: load %names
probe names
== ["John" "Dave" "Jane" "Bob" "Sue" "Sarah" "Mikhail" "Rudolf" "Nenad"]
type? names ;== block!
```

Because code can have a complex structure, you should use `save` to store code into a file. This file can then immediately be executed with `do`. Here is a simple example:

```
save %code.red [ Red[] print "Hello from saved Red" ]
do %code.red
;== Hello from saved Red
```

The file can be immediately interpreted with `do`, or you can load it first in a variable to manipulate it, and then `do` it:

```
code: load %code.red
do code
```

The following example defines a function, stores it in a file, and then loads and executes it:

```
code: [appin: func [input /local str] [str: "-" append str input]]
save %codef.red code
blk: load %codef.red
;== [appin: func [input /local str] [str: "-" append str input]]
do blk
;== func [input /local str][str: "-" append str input]
appin "a"
;== "-a"
appin "b"
;== "-ab"
:appin
;== func [input /local str][str: "-ab" append str input]
```

The `do` word interprets the code and defines the function in the program's memory. The local `str` variable has not been initialized with `copy`, so subsequent calls to the `appin` function make it accumulate the input. The `:appin` word gets the value of the `appin` word, which is the function's definition.

=> Now answer question 5 in the *Questions* section.

Saving and loading the console history

Sometimes, when you have tried things out in the console, you will like to keep a file trace of what you have experimented with, perhaps to save portions of it later in a source file. This can be done with the following simple console command:

```
save %history system/console/history
```

Here, `history` is just the file you want to store them in (this could be any other name).

From Version 0.6.4 onward, the `history` command is preserved between sessions, but if you would like to start a session with an older file with commands, you can retrieve the history like this:

```
system/console/history: load %history
```

Downloading currency exchange rates

At the end of the *Reading and writing files* section, we learned how to download files from the internet. Let's use this knowledge to download some currency exchange rates data from Floatrates (`http://www.floatrates.com/`). As one of its many services, this website offers the current exchange rates of any currency compared to most common currencies. These rates can be obtained in XML or JSON format. For example, the URL `http://www.floatrates.com/daily/USD.xml` shows a spreadsheet layout of currencies compared to the US dollar (USD):

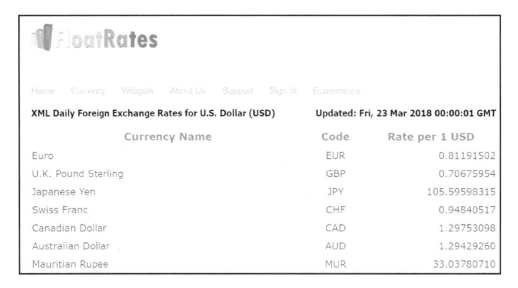

For example, today (Mar 23, 2018) it shows that 1 USD is worth 0.81191502 Euros (EUR). The resource for this nice web page is an XML file, in which all exchange rate data are stored, in our case, `USD.xml`.

We now know how to download this data and store it in a local `rates.xml` file for further processing:

```
;-- see Chapter07/currency-rates.red:
write %rates.xml read http://www.floatrates.com/daily/USD.xml
```

You can examine the format of the `rates.xml` file in any text editor. The header line `<?xml version="1.0" encoding="utf-8"?>` confirms us that it is in XML format.

The same info is also available in JSON format (`http://www.floatrates.com/daily/USD.json`), although with a less fancy layout.

Using query string parameters

What if we want to know the rates for a date in the past, say, March 15? The website shows us that these rates can be obtained at `http://www.floatrates.com/historical-exchange-rates.html?currency_date=2018-03-15base_currency_code=USDformat_type=xml`. This URL uses query string parameters to pass the date, currency code, and format type to the FloatRates web service.

We can make our script flexible by storing these parameters in variables and asking the user for the specific values he/she is interested in. We then build the complete URL by applying `rejoin` on a block, fitting in, and joining all parts of the URL together:

```
;-- see Chapter07/currency-rates2.red:
url-base: http://www.floatrates.com/historical-exchange-rates.html?
curr-code: ask "Rates for which currency (format like USD)? "
curr-date: ask "Rates from which date (YYYY-MM-DD)? "
url: rejoin [url-base "&currency_date=" curr-date "&base_currency_code="
curr-code    "&format_type=xml"]
rates: read url
write %rates_hist.xml rates
```

=> Now answer question 6 in the *Questions* section.

Both XML and JSON, as well as other formats, can be handled quite easily with the Red `parse` dialect. In the next chapter, we'll analyse this data to extract the relevant information.

Summary

In this chapter, we've learned how to work with files and folders from the REPL and from within Red code. We saw how to interactively ask the user for a file or a folder, and how easy it is to `read` and `write` files, even in binary format or from the internet. When working with code, it is preferable to use `save` and `load`. We ended the chapter by downloading currency exchange data, to be processed in the next chapter.

Questions

1. Write the contents of the `contacts` series out to a `contacts3.txt` file with `/lines`. What is different now?

2. Try out `write/part` with `20` as an argument. What does it do?

3. `write/seek %file new-text n` (where n is a number) is used to replace the text in `%file` starting at position *n*+1. Try this out for the `contacts` series and replace `John` in the first item with `Adam`.

4. Use `save` and `load` to store and read our `contacts` series in a file.

5. Rewrite the `appin` function with a `copy ""` and call it several times to see the difference.

6. Write a script to ask the user the currency and the format type she/he is interested in (XML or JSON). Here, you have to use the `http://www.floatrates.com/daily/USD.xml` format, which doesn't use query string parameters. Try it out by obtaining data in JSON format. Hint: Use `probe` to see whether your URL is correct!

8
Parsing Data

One of the key focus areas in software development today is working on and analyzing (big) data streams. Every programming language needs to have some support for these kinds of tasks. Most languages use **regular expressions** (in short, **regex** (`https://www.regular-expressions.info/examples.html`)) for such tasks. These expressions match patterns in string data using a specialized formal syntax, which often comes across as an awkward addition to the code.

Red takes a different approach. While Red offers all series operations for working with data, it also has its own **domain-specific language** (**DSL**) or **dialect** called **parse**, specifically built for text and data processing. The parsing engine is implemented in Red/System. It has its own specific words and syntax, but embedded in other Red code it feels very natural. Parse code itself is much more human-readable and maintainable than regex. It is more powerful, not limited to string parsing, and it performs better.

In this chapter, we'll explore how to work with parse, which is an indispensable tool for any Red developer.

The following topics will be covered:

- The bitset! datatype
- How parse works
- Searching, extracting, and changing
- More features and examples

Technical requirements

You'll find the code for this chapter at `https://github.com/PacktPublishing/Learn-Red-Fundamentals-of-Red/tree/master/Chapter08`. If you have installed Red as indicated in `Chapter 2`, *Setting Up for Development*, you are good to go. You can work on Windows, macOS, or Linux. You can type or paste any code in the Red console to see its results, or you can start using an editor such as Visual Studio Code.

The bitset! datatype

This datatype was made specifically so that parse could work efficiently with strings consisting of Unicode values. It is used to store an arbitrary set of characters as Boolean values, that is, as a set of bits.

A value of the `bitset!` type is created with `make bitset!`, accepting a character, string, an integer (within the Unicode codepoint range), or a series of these values, such as these:

```
;-- see Chapter08/bitsets.red:
make bitset! #"R"            ;== make bitset! #{0000000000000000000000020}
make bitset! "Red"          ;== make bitset!
#{00000000000000000000020000C}
make bitset! [108 "Red" #"R"]  ;== make bitset!
#{000000000000000000000020000C08}
```

Note that a bitset value is represented in hexadecimal format. A convenient shortcut function that does the same thing is `charset`. So, for example, the last line could also be written as `charset [108 "Red" #"R"]` (compare the bitset binary value to see that they are equal).

Now we can make a bitset to store all vowels:

```
vowel: charset "aeiou" ;== make bitset! #{0000000000000000000000000000444104}
```

We can use that to search efficiently for the first vowel in a string, like this:

```
str: "dog"
find str vowel      ;== "og"
```

(Remember here, that `find` returns the series starting with the value of the match.)

The following is a charset to store all digits:

```
digit: charset "0123456789"
```

Another way to represent this is as a *range* with a – between either two character or two integer values:

```
digit: charset [#"0" - #"9"]
```

=> Now answer question 1 from the *Questions* section.

If you have found the answer to this question, here is how to store all letters. We can do this in two ways. First as:

```
letter: charset [#"a" - #"z" #"A" - #"Z"]
```

We can also use the `union` word:

```
letter: union lower upper
```

where `lower` and `upper` are defined respectively as:

```
lower: charset [#"a" - #"z"]
upper: charset [#"A" - #"Z"]
```

=> Now answer questions 2 and 3 from the *Questions* section.

The other set functions can be used as well.

The following `ws` bitset stores the whitespace characters—`ws: charset reduce [space tab cr lf]`. Use `not` to make complementary bitsets—`non-digit: charset [`**not**` "0123456789"]`.

To create an empty bitset with a memory allocation of 100 bits, do the following:

```
make bitset! 100 ;== make bitset! #{00000000000000000000000000}
```

This is because size is rounded to a multiple of 8 and there are 26 hex digits for 104 characters.

A bitset can be expanded by using `append`, as in these examples:

```
bs1: make bitset! "A"    ;== make bitset! #{000000000000000040}
append bs1 "Z"           ;== make bitset! #{000000000000000040000020}
```

The memory allocation of `bs1` is automatically expanded to its new size.

Understanding how parse works

The way parse works is quite straightforward. It's a function that takes an input to parse, and a set of rules to parse the input with—`parse input [rules]`

The input is the data that needs to be processed; it can be *any series* value. This is in most cases *a string*, perhaps coming from a web page, an XML or JSON or other type of file, or a spreadsheet, but it could also be a block with values, a binary value, or even code.

Parse searches the input and tries to pattern match it from start to finish with the rules. If the complete input until the end matches the rules, `true` is returned; if not, parse returns `false`. In fact, the rules block can be a complete subprogram, extracting information from the input, and processing that as well:

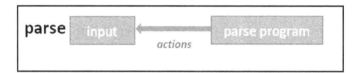

First parse examples

Let's start with some simple examples, where we have a product code that starts with the letter combination `XY`, followed by a digit, which we defined as a bitset `digit` in the previous section, for example, `"XY6"`. We can parse this input with the rule block `["XY" digit]`:

```
;-- see Chapter08/how-parse-works.red:
parse "XY6" ["XY" digit]        ;== true
```

This works as follows. Look inside `"XY6"` from left to right, find a `"XY"`, if found, then find one digit. If this is found and we are at the end of the input, return `true`. But in the code `"XY67"` there are two digits. The end of the input was not reached, and parse returns `false`:

```
parse "XY67" ["XY" digit]    ;== false
```

We can make it match by specifying the number of digits, like this:

```
parse "XY67" ["XY" 2 digit] ;== true
```

Instead of a number, a range such as `2 4 digit` could also be specified, meaning two to four digits may be present. If 0 is used as the start value, then the item following the range is optional.

Note that parsing is, by default, case insensitive

```
parse "xy67" ["XY" 2 4 digit]  ;== true
```

If you want the input and pattern to have the exact same case, use the `/case` refinement:

```
parse/case "xy67" ["XY" 2 4 digit]  ;== false
```

If you only need to parse a part of the input, use `/part` with the length of the parse:

```
parse/part "xy67" ["XY"] 2  ;== true
parse/part "xy67" ["XY"] 3  ;== false
```

Using some and any

If the number of digits is unspecified (but there is at least one digit), we can use `some`:

```
parse "XY67" ["XY" some digit]      ;== true
parse "XY" ["XY" some digit]        ;== false
parse "XY2915" ["XY" some digit]    ;== true
```

`any` can be used instead of `some`, matching the pattern even when there is no digit in the input:

```
parse "XY67" ["XY" any digit]    ;== true
parse "XY" ["XY" any digit]      ;== true
```

To summarize, `some` is 1 or more, `any` is 0 or more.

`any` and `some` only apply to the first item that follows them. For example:

```
parse "XXY" [some "X" "Y"]       ;== true
parse "XYXY" [some "X" "Y"]      ;== false
```

In the last line, the second `"X"` is not matched. To make this work, we could use the following:

```
parse "XYXY" [some ["X" "Y"]]    ;== true
```

Or even simpler:

```
parse "XYXY" [some "XY"]         ;== true
```

For such trivial examples it is overkill, but in more elaborate examples the code is more readable and flexible by using words, such as this:

```
input: "XY2915"
rules: ["XY" some digit]
parse input [rules]        ;==true
```

Matching positions

Parse *pattern matches* (or, in general, *evaluates the rules*) from left to right. You can visualize this with a position arrow, which points before the input at the start of the rules block:

When rules are matched, the parse position is moved. After the first pattern we get:

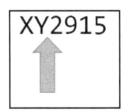

Then the some digit pattern processes the rest of the input, the parse position is at the end of the input, and true is returned:

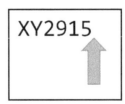

If the input contains one (or more) spaces, there is no match:

```
parse "XY 2915" ["XY" some digit]          ;== false
```

To make it match again, use `space`:

```
parse "XY 2915" ["XY" space some digit]    ;== true
```

Or you could just skip the space character (or any character for that matter) with `skip`:

```
parse "XY 2915" ["XY" skip some digit]     ;== true
```

If you want to skip several characters or a range, use a number or a number range before `skip`:

```
parse "XYabc2915" ["XY" 3 skip some digit]     ;== true
parse "XY2915" ["XY" 0 3 skip some digit]      ;== true
```

When you are interested in only one pattern in your input (such as ID in the following example), use `skip` like this:

```
program: {
    ID: 121.34
    Version: 1.2.3-5.6
    Description: "This program calculates ..."
}
id: [3 digit dot 2 digit]
parse program [some [ id | skip]]    ;== true
probe value    ;== "121.34"
```

Note that `dot` is a built-in character—dot `;== #"."`.

As we will see in the following section, if we need the value of ID, we can copy it to a variable `value` as follows:

```
parse program [some [copy value id | skip]] ;== true
probe value ;== "121.34"
```

Choosing with |

If the starting character is either an `X` or a `Y`, such as in `X123` or `Y108`, we can use `"X"` | `"Y"`, where | stands for or, so the expression reads like `"X"` or `"Y"`:

```
xy: ["X" | "Y"]
parse "X123" [xy some digit]    ;== true
parse "Y108" [xy some digit]    ;== true
```

| can be used for a small number of choices, but if there are more than a few choices, it is better to make a charset and use that in the pattern:

```
uz: charset "UVWXYZ"
parse "X123" [uz some digit]     ;== true
parse "V456" [uz some digit]     ;== true
```

=> Now answer questions 4 and 5 from the *Questions* section.

Searching, extracting, and changing

Let's now try something more than just an example. In the previous chapter, we read in some currency exchange rates, in particular how much one **USD** (**US Dollar**) is worth in other currencies. In this section, we'll extract the exchange rates and currencies, learn how to use variables, copy data, and execute code when a match is found.

Working with variables – to, thru, and copy

The exchange rates file was named `rates.xml`, and when we look at its contents in an editor, it consists of a number of `<item>` XML tags, each containing an exchange rate, such as this:

```
<item>
    <title>1 USD = 0.81191502 EUR</title>
    <link>http://www.floatrates.com/usd/eur/</link>
    <description>1 U.S. Dollar = 0.81191502 Euro</description>
    <pubDate>Fri, 23 Mar 2018 00:00:01 GMT</pubDate>
    <baseCurrency>USD</baseCurrency>
    <baseName>U.S. Dollar</baseName>
    <targetCurrency>EUR</targetCurrency>
    <targetName>Euro</targetName>
    <exchangeRate>0.81191502</exchangeRate>
</item>
<item>
    <title>1 USD = 0.70675954 GBP</title>
      ...
</item>
```

We see that this contains all the information we need; in fact, only `<title>` is enough.

Let's see how we could parse that string:

```
rate: "<title>1 USD = 0.81191502 EUR</title>"
```

To move the parse position pointer just before a string `str`, you use the `to` rule—`to str`.

We can show this by inserting a variable `pos`, which represents the rest of the series at that point (don't forget the `:`). The position in the series is then given by `index? pos`:

```
;-- see Chapter08/searching-and-changing.red:
parse rate [to "<title>" pos:]  ;== false
pos                             ;== "<title>1 USD = 0.81191502 EUR</title>"
index? pos                      ;== 1
```

To move the parse position pointer just after the string `str`, you use the `thru` rule—`thru str`.

If we apply this to `rate`, we get the following:

```
parse rate [thru "<title>" pos:]   ;== false
pos                                ;== "1 USD = 0.81191502 EUR</title>"
index? pos                         ;== 8
```

In our case, the exchange rate information we want is inside the `<title>` tag. So we want to parse just after `"<title>"`, until just before `"</title>"`.

Let's try the following:

```
parse rate [thru "<title>" to "</title>"]
```

But this gives `false`, because we didn't parse to the end of the input. To go all the way through to the end making `parse` return `true`, use the dedicated `end` word:

```
parse rate [thru "<title>" to "</title>" to end]
```

Combining `thru` and `to`, we can also get the positions:

```
parse rate [thru "<title>" pos1: to "</title>" pos2: to end] ;== true
pos1                                ;== "1 USD = 0.81191502 EUR</title>"
index? pos1                         ;== 8
pos2                                ;== "</title>"
index? pos2                         ;== 30
```

However, this is not yet very useful. How do we get the data in between the `<title>` and `</title>` tags? This is done with the `copy` word:

```
parse rate [thru "<title>" copy data to "</title>" to end]    ;== true
```

Now `data` contains what we need:

```
print data    ;1 USD = 0.81191502 EUR
```

(Use `probe` instead of `print` to see the type of `data`; here, it is a simple string.)

`copy` is always followed by a variable (here, `data`) and precedes a match rule (here, `to "</title>"`).

`copy` extracts the whole matched string. When you need only the first character, use `set`:

```
parse rate [thru "<title>" set data to "</title>" (print data) to end]
; 1 ;== true
```

Now try to parse the `data` string to extract the exchange rate `0.81191502` yourself (see question 6 in the *Questions* section). If you didn't find it, make sure you understand the solution.

Executing code on a match

Inside a parse rule, we can provide code that will only be executed when a match is found. This code must be enclosed within parentheses ( ).

For example, here we simply print out the `data` variable, after the `to` rule has found a match:

```
parse rate [thru "<title>" copy data to "</title>" (print data) to end]
;1 USD = 0.81191502 EUR ;== true
```

Now let's turn to the complete rates file again—`rates: read %rates.xml`.

To parse through the complete file extracting information from each <title> tag, we can use `any` from the previous section as follows:

```
any [thru "<title>" copy data to "</title>"]
```

Each time it finds a <title> tag, the condition becomes `true` and the data is copied. Verify for yourself that `all` will not work here; why would that be?

To store each data item, we need to use code to append this item to a previously declared series, usd:

```
usd: copy []
parse rates [ any [thru "<title>" copy data to "</title>" (append usd
data)] ]
usd     ;== [{XML Daily Foreign Exchange Rates for U.S. Dollar (USD)} "1 USD
= 0.81191502 EUR" "1 USD = 0.70675954 GBP" "1 USD = 0.94840517 CHF" "1 USD
= 1.29753098 CAD" "1 USD = 1.294292...
```

We see that usd now contains strings with the exchange rates. The first string is the title of the XML file itself, which we can eliminate by positioning it right before the first usable data item:

```
parse rates [
    thru </lastBuildDate>
    any [thru "<title>" copy data to "</title>" (append usd data)]
]
```

Now usd is as follows:

```
["1 USD = 0.81191502 EUR" "1 USD = 0.70675954 GBP" "1 USD = 0.94840517 CHF"
"1 USD = 1.29753098 CAD" "1 USD = 1.29429260 AUD" "1 USD = 105.59598315
JPY" "1 USD = 114.07517952 ...
```

This is not the most efficient form to contain this data. Perhaps we would like our data in this form:

```
[ "EUR" 0.81191502 "GPB" 0.70675954 ... ]
```

We can see that this information is contained in the <targetCurrency> and <exchangeRate> tags. With the tools you have acquired now, this is easy to do.

=> Answer question 8 from the *Questions* section then also answer question 9.

Having extracted the data in a series, we can now use all other Red tools at our disposal to work with that data.

The variables can be used in more flexible ways together; they are known in other pieces of parse code, as this example shows:

```
parse "xxxyyy" [copy letters some "x" (n: length? letters) n "y"] ;== true
letters         ;== "xxx"
```

The match of `some` `"x"` is copied out into `letters`. The length of the `letters` word sets the number of following `y` characters that are going to be matched.

`copy` can also be used on other types. Here is an example of `copy` used on a binary value:

```
parse #{FFFFDECAFBAD000000} [
    2 #{FF}
    copy data to #{00}
    some #{00}
] ;== true
data ;== #{DECAFBAD}
```

Changing data – change, remove, and insert

Suppose we want to change the `<title>` tag in the `rate` string to `<rate>`. This is also something you can do with `parse`, using the `change` word:

```
parse rate [to "<title>" change "<title>" "<rate>"]      ;== false
rate       ;== "<rate>1 USD = 0.81191502 EUR</title>"
```

Although parse didn't go through to the end (it returned `false`), the `rate` string has been changed!

Just to show how you can make a parse program more flexible by defining new words, we rewrite the same example:

```
start-tag: "<title>"
change-tag: "<rate>"
find-tag: [to start-tag]
replace-tag: [change start-tag change-tag]
parse rate [find-tag replace-tag]

do-action: [find-tag replace-tag]
parse rate do-action
rate ;== "<rate>1 USD = 0.81191502 EUR</title>"
```

=> Now change both tags `<title>` and `</title>` in the original string, by using two rules (see question 7 in the *Questions* section).

Apart from changing, you can also remove part of the input or insert something in the input at the parse position. Here are some examples:

```
rate: "<title>1 USD = 0.81191502 EUR</title>"
parse rate [to "<title>" remove "<title>"]    ;== false
rate                                          ;== "1 USD = 0.81191502
EUR</title>"

rate: "<title>1 USD = 0.81191502 EUR</title>"
parse rate [to "<title>" insert "NEW"]        ;== false
rate                                          ;== "NEW<title>1 USD = 0.81191502
EUR</title>"
```

More features and examples

The parse dialect has a lot more useful features and functionalities. In this section, we discuss some more examples, so that you get a feeling for what is possible.

Using end

Remember our vowels example from *The bitset! datatype* section?

```
;-- see Chapter08/more-features.red:
vowel: charset "aeiou"
str: "dog"
find str vowel    ;== "og"
```

Using parse we can write this as follows:

```
parse str [ to vowel to end]     ;== true
parse "xyz" [ to vowel to end]   ;== false
```

The end word, which exists only in the parse dialect, returns true when the current position pointer is at the end of the input.

Building special languages

Email addresses are of the form `host@domain`, where `domain` is a `"."` followed by a three-letter domain name, and `host` can contain letters, digits, and one or more `"-"`, such as `dtrump@whitehouse.org`. We can build a pattern from the ground up to describe the components of an email pattern, like this:

```
digit: charset "0123456789"
letter: charset [#"a" - #"z" #"A" - #"Z"]
dash: charset "-"
email-char: union union letter dash digit
email-word: [some email-char]
host: [email-word]
domain: [email-word some [dot email-word]]
email: [host "@" domain]

parse "dtrump@whitehouse.org" email          ;== true
parse "john-locke@lost.island.org" email     ;== true
```

You can see how parse can be used to gradually build a kind of mini-language or DSL (domain-specific language) to search for patterns. For example, here is a nice tutorial that builds a parse language for executing calculator expressions (`http://www.red-by-example.org/parse.html#1`).

Changing a rule on the fly

A parsing rule can be changed while it is being applied, as the following example shows:

```
rule: ["x" | "y"]
parse "xyyxqyyxz" [
    some [
        rule
    |
        "q" (append rule [ | "z" ])
    ]
]   ;== true
```

When the letter q is found, the rule is enhanced so that it also matches the letter z. That's why parse returns true in this case.

Parsing blocks and code

Parsing is not only used for string data, it can also be applied on blocks, including Red code. Let's concentrate here on what is specific for blocks, particularly the use of words and types in the match rules.

The following parse statement returns true:

parse ["x"] ["z" | "x" | "y"] ;== true, but this statement parse [x] [z | x | y] gives us a Script Error: PARSE – invalid rule or usage of rule: z. Why is this? Red doesn't know the types of x, y, and z; it has to consider them as words, and when they don't have a value Red returns an error.

However, we can make this work like this:

```
parse [x] ['z | 'x | 'y] ;== true
```

By indicating with ' that x, y, and z are words, Red can make sense of the statement.

=> Now answer question 10 from the *Questions* section.

When parsing blocks, you can make use of type indications in the matching rules, as shown in this example:

```
parse [hi Red world] [3 word!]    ;== true
```

The collect and keep words can be used to collect in a block those items that are matched by keep. For instance, in the following block we keep all integers and collect returns them as a block:

```
input: [13 "Red" 42 a-word %file 108 3.14]
parse input [ collect[ some[ keep integer! | any-type!] ] ]
;== [13 42 108]
```

Finally, here is a complete example where parse works on a code snippet. Suppose we have the following piece of code:

```
code: [
    if x < n [
        print {x is smaller than n}
    ]
    print {in the middle of the code}
    probe "true"
    probe n
    if n = y [
        probe "n and y are equal"
    ]
]
```

We want to extract to a `result` series, all occurrences of a word followed by a string, such as `print {...}` or `probe "true"`. We can accomplish this with the following rule:

```
result: []
;-- if word-string match, append to result
rule: [ start: word! string! finish:
    ( append result copy/part start finish )
]
```

Notice how `start` and `finish` are used to delimit the word/string combination. The following parse code does what we want:

```
parse code [
    some [
        rule          ; (1)
    |
        ahead block!  ; (2)
        into rule     ; (3)
    |
        skip          ; (4)
    ]
]
```

In line `(1)`, we try to match the word/string rule. When matched, the word and the string are appended to `result`. If there is no match, and we find a block `[ ]` in line `(2)`, we go into it in line `(3)` and apply the rule. `ahead` looks for a match to the right, but does not advance the parse pointer.

If there was no word/string match and no block, we would simply `skip` to the next position with line `(4)`.

The resulting series `result` contains all occurrences in the code where a word was followed by a string—`probe result` shows us the following:

```
[
    print "x is smaller than n"
    print "in the middle of the code"
    probe "true"
    probe "n and y are equal"
]
```

This is even executable code—`do result` gives us the following output:

```
x is smaller than n
in the middle of the code
"true"
"n and y are equal"
; == "n and y are equal"
```

Debugging parse

Sometimes, you need some help to see how the parse process is working. A simple measure is to include a `print` or `probe` statement with certain matches, such as when parsing the rate string in the *Searching, extracting, and changing* section:

```
rate: "<title>1 USD = 0.81191502 EUR</title>"
parse rate [thru "<title>" copy data to "</title>" (probe data) thru ">"]
;"1 USD = 0.81191502 EUR"
;== true
```

Or you could simply print out:

`(print "found a </title>")`, to indicate that a match was found.

Let's apply this to the last example from the previous section:

```
rule: [start: word! string! finish:
    (
        print ["-->" start]
        print ["<--" finish]
        append result copy/part start finish
    )
]
```

This prints out the following:

```
--> print x is smaller than n
 <--
 --> print in the middle of the code probe true probe n if n = y probe n
and y are equal
 <-- probe true probe n if n = y probe n and y are equal
 --> probe true probe n if n = y probe n and y are equal
 <-- probe n if n = y probe n and y are equal
 --> probe n and y are equal
 <--
 ;== true
```

We can get a similar, but even more detailed output of each match by replacing `parse` with `parse-trace`:

```
parse-trace rate [thru "<title>" copy data to "</title>" (probe data) thru
">"]

-->
match: [thru "<title>" copy data to "</title>" (probe dat
input: "<title>1 USD = 0.81191502 EUR</title>"
-->
==> matched
<--
match: ["<title>" copy data to "</title>" (probe data) th
input: "1 USD = 0.81191502 EUR</title>"
-->
-->
==> matched
<--
<--
match: [data to "</title>" (probe data) thru ">"]
input: "</title>"
"1 USD = 0.81191502 EUR"
match: [to "</title>" (probe data) thru ">"]
input: "</title>"
-->
==> matched
<--
return: true
== true
```

Much more can be done with the `/trace` refinement:

```
parse/trace input rules callback
```

`callback` is a function that responds to events in the parsing process and can be used to provide tracing, statistical, and debugging information.

Summary

Now you have learned to perform simple and the more complex tasks of recognizing, analyzing, and manipulating data by using parse. We first got to know the `bitset!` datatype and its handy charset equivalent. Then, we learned how to parse with to and thru, extract data (with copy), and change data. We saw how we can attach code to a rule to be executed when it matches. Finally, we explored how to parse blocks and code, and how to get a detailed output of how parse works in a specific case.

This chapter was not exhaustive, some other words exist in parse which we haven't talked about. In fact, the parse dialect deserves a book on its own.

Questions

1. Make a bitset to store all lowercase letters and another for all uppercase letters.
2. Use `union` to make a bitset storing all alphanumerical characters.
3. Use `union` to make a bitset storing all characters used in hexadecimal numbers.
4. Make a rules pattern `integer` to match with integer numbers, starting optionally with a + or - sign.
5. Make a pattern that matches the following product codes: `"#ABC-nnnn"` or `"#XYZ-nnnn"`, where `nnnn` is a four-digit pattern.
6. Try for yourself to parse the `data` string to extract the exchange rate `0.81191502`. (Hint: use `some` and the `letter` charset.)
7. Starting with `rate: "<title>1 USD = 0.81191502 EUR</title>"`, change both tags to `<rate>` tags, by using two rules.
8. Use parse and the code within it to obtain the exchange rate info in this form: `[ "EUR" 0.81191502 "GPB" 0.70675954 ... ]`

9. Parse strings that contain two different letters (in random order and numbers). The parse must return true and print out each letter it finds.

10. Rewrite the following code so that it works with a block [x x x y y y]:

```
parse "xxxyyy" [copy letters some "x" (n: length? letters) n "y"]
;== true
letters          ;== "xxx"
```

Composing Visual Interfaces

9

Red comes with a built-in, cross-platform, graphical capability called **View**. This is unique among current programming languages. For most of them this is not a priority, and when it is possible, it is tedious and leads to verbose code. Here, Red really shines. You'll be amazed by the elegance with which you can build complex interactive screens in a simple declarative way.

As of version 0.6.3, Windows and macOS are fully supported, the other platforms (Linux, Android, iOS) are partly ready and scheduled for the near future.

Red relies on *native widgets*. It binds on each platform to the default native GUI API available, so that users get to see familiar graphics. On Linux, **Visual Interface Dialect** (**VID**) will rely on the well-known GTK graphical toolkit.

We'll build further on several examples from the previous chapters, to download exchange rates and develop an interactive contact maintenance app.

The following topics will be covered in this chapter:

- Structuring an interface
- A faces walkthrough
- Events and actors
- Basic contacts app
- An introduction to the draw dialect

Technical requirements

You'll find the code for this chapter at `https://github.com/PacktPublishing/Learn-Red-Fundamentals-of-Red/tree/master/Chapter09`. If you have installed Red as indicated in `Chapter 2`, *Setting Up for Development*, you are good to go. You can work on Windows, macOS, or Linux. You can type or paste any code in the Red console to see its results, or you can start using an editor, such as Visual Studio Code.

Structuring an interface

View, the graphical interface engine, is completely written in Red and Red/System. The following diagram shows how View is structured with the help of three other parts in a bit more detail:

- **VID**: The Visual Interface Dialect
- **Draw**: The dialect to draw two-dimensional shapes
- **React**: This is an engine that makes the whole system automatically and fully reactive to the user or system events

You can check their relationship in the following screenshot:

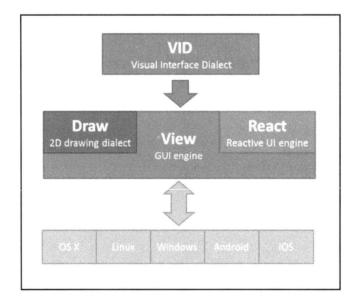

The VID dialect contains a lot of words, and we'll cover them systematically so that you don't get bewildered. In this section, we'll talk about the basic window, container, and layout settings. But to get you started with some fundamentals, we'll build a screen interface for the *Downloading currency and exchange rates* script that we made in `Chapter 7, Working with Files`.

First example – a screen for downloading exchange rates

Transforming the `currency-rates2.red` script from `Chapter 7`, *Working with Files*, into a screen app is quite easy. We draw the widgets (the text, input fields, and a button) and provide code to execute when the button is pressed. We'll present you with the complete script called `currency-rates-gui.red`, and then explain how it works in detail.

Running the example

Follow these steps to run the program:

- First run the app to see how it works—from the Red console, go to the folder where the script is, for example, `cd %/E/Red/code/ch9`, then type in the following—do `%currency-rates-gui.red`
- Or, first compile the script with, `red -r currency-rates-gui.red`, and then run it with, `./currency-rates-gui`

(Double-clicking the EXE in Windows will show the app window on a black console background. To avoid this, compile with `red -r -t Windows` or `red -c -t Windows`.)

The following screen appears:

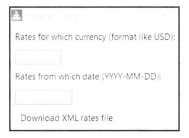

Fill in, for example, **USD** and the exchange rates, date (click with the mouse cursor to go the next field), click the **Download XML rates file** button, and after a few seconds the text **SUCCESS!** appears, and the XML file is downloaded:

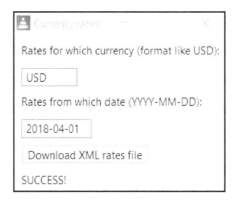

 TAB key functionality for jumping from one field to another is not yet implemented in Windows, so the user must use the mouse for now. This will be solved in the forthcoming release, 0.6.4.

Examining the code

Here is the complete script, which we'll now discuss:

```
;-- see Chapter09/currency-rates-gui.red:
Red [
    title: "Downloading currency exchange rates"
    needs: 'view                            (1)
]

url-base: http://www.floatrates.com/historical-exchange-rates.html?
download-rates: does [                      (2)
    url: rejoin [url-base "&currency_date=" curr-date/text
"&base_currency_code=" curr-code/text "&format_type=xml"]
    rates: read url
    write %rates-hist.xml rates
    out/text: "SUCCESS!"                     (3)
]

view [                                       (4)
    title "Currency rates"                   (5)
    below                                    (6)
```

```
    text "Rates for which currency (format like USD):"   (7)
    curr-code: field                    (8)
    text "Rates from which date (YYYY-MM-DD):"
    curr-date: field 100x25             (9)
    button "Download XML rates file" [download-rates]    (10)
    out: text ""                        (11)
]
```

In line (1), we see a piece of code that must always be present in the Red header of a View app, needs: 'view, which tells the interpreter to load the View engine, or the compiler to include it during compilation (the ' is optional). Inside the Red GUI console, View is already present, so you can paste a view block in it and the window will be shown.

In line (5), we specify the window's title. In line (6), below specifies that all widgets are to be placed below one another. In line (7), the first text that has to appear on the screen is declared as a string.

In line (8), curr-code: field, an input field, is defined with the name curr-code. The date field in line (9) has a size 100x25 specified. On line (10), a button widget is declared. Notice that the text on widgets such as text or button is simply the string that follows it. The button also has a [download-rates] block, which is a code section that is executed when the button is clicked (its default event). Finally, in line (11), an output field is declared as empty and given the name out.

The download-rates is a simple does function defined in line (2). It contains our previous download code, but notice how the content of the input fields is retrieved with /text—curr-code/text and curr-date/text. The output field's content is set in line (3) with out/text: "SUCCESS!".

It is that easy to compose a screen and attach event code to it in Red!

=> Now solve question 1 from the *Questions* section.

Building a layout

The UI code starts from line `(4)`, `view [ ... ]`. The `view` is a function that expects a window description as an argument. Note that this window description is just a code block using VID words. You could give it a name such as `win`, build this block with `append` or other code, and when you're ready, do view `win`. The `view []` displays a minimal GUI window:

```
win: []
; build up win with statements like append win [title "Currency rates"]
view win
```

This allows for dynamically building screens based upon user input or events. There is also a built-in `layout` word in VID. Give your `layout` a name, and define it inside the block that follows, like this:

```
lay1: layout [a: area cyan 200x200]
```

`layout` builds a tree of `face!` objects from the block that specifies them. Then, you display it with `view`, which works on these object trees, `view lay1`. In fact, `view [...]` is just an abbreviation for `view layout [...]`.

In most of our examples, we'll stick to the static way of building our screens, but for defining menus, we'll use this way of working.

Faces and actions

The widgets such as `text`, `field`, and `button` are called *faces* in Red. The details of a face, such as its size, color, or text, are called its *facets*. For example, in `field 100x25` the pair value `100x25` is a facet describing the size (width x height) of the field (Red knows that because a pair value with a field is always a size). The order in which the facets are written does not matter. Faces can be given a name so that their properties can be used or manipulated in code, as we saw with the `curr-code`, `curr-date`, and `out` faces.

What is displayed by `view` is in fact also a face type, namely, the `window`. A program can contain multiple views, which by default appear as successive windows when the previous window is closed.

Faces are placed inside a *container* (in this case, the window), and they are placed following a certain *layout*. In our example:

- `title "Currency rates"` is a *container* command describing the container window
- `below` is a *layout* command dictating that all of the following faces will appear below each other

The block of commands that is optionally attached to a face is called an *action facet*, or in short, an *actor*. This is code that will be executed when a certain *event* takes place, for example, clicking a button initiates the download of the XML file. An event is given the prefix `on`, such as `on-click`. Most faces respond to a default event, such as `on-click` for a `button`. For default events, you do not need to specify their name, but if you want other events, you'll have to indicate these.

A face can be `visible` or not, and when it is, it can be `enabled` or disabled. You can get that status with the functions `face/visible?` and `face/enabled?` (see question 4 in the *Questions* section).

Faces are implemented as *objects*. To see their complexity, print their contents to the console. For example, when `bt` is the name of a `button`, use `print bt` or `probe bt` in its action facet (see question 2 in the *Questions* section).

Two-way binding

User interface screens and all they contain are updated automatically in real time when their properties change. A *two-way binding* exists between faces and facets. When either one of them changes, the other follows accordingly. We won't use it in our examples, but if you as a developer want to control when the screen is updated, you need to do the following:

- Turn the `auto-sync` option off—`system/view/auto-sync?: off`
- Use the `show` function such as `show face` to update the widget

=> Find out in question 3 from the *Questions* section how to code a button to close the window.

Container settings – view

These are settings that describe the look and feel of the container facet (the window). We already used `title`. Here are some common settings that can be combined in any order (paste the code in the Red console, and play with it):

- `view [ `**`size`**` 350x125]` allows windows with different sizes (width x height)
- `view [ backdrop blue]` creates a window with a blue background

Changing an app's icon

The default Red window *icon* (displaying the towers of Hanoi) can be replaced with your own `.ico` file as follows:

```
;-- see Chapter09/icon.red:
Red [
    needs: 'view
    icon: %gaming.ico
]
view []
```

This window displays as:

But to see this new icon, the app must be compiled as `red -r icon.red`. This also works for the icon of a non-GUI app shown in the app-tray.

View's refinements

`view` can also have one or several refinements. Their details are described in blocks that come after the main `view` block, as you can see in the following schema of a general `view` block:

```
view/refine1/refine2 [
    container settings
    layout commands
    face1 facets [action facet]
    face2 facets [action facet]
    ...
][details refine1][details refine2]
```

To determine where a window must appear on the screen, use the `options` refinement with a block giving the `offset` value, like this:

```
;-- see Chapter09/container-layout.red:
view/options [
][offset: 400x100]
```

You might have noticed that a standard window is not resizable or maximizable. To accomplish this, we need the `flags` refinement with the `resize` word:

```
view/flags [
][resize]
```

These flags can be combined as in this example, where the window is resizable and modal:

```
view/flags/options [
][modal resize][offset: 400x100]
```

Modal means that the window is displayed on top of the parent window, which is disabled as long as the modal window is shown. In other words, a modal window demands your attention.

There are other flags such as `no-title`, `no-border`, `no-min`, `no-max`, and `no-buttons`. Their names give away what they do. Combine them to make minimal windows when appropriate.

Here is an example of the use of these flags:

```
;-- see Chapter09/digital-clock.red:
time-now: to string! now/time
view/flags [
    title "Red Time"
    show-time: text font-size 14 font-color red time-now
]
[modal popup]
```

This displays the following window:

It also shows the use of `font-size` and `font-color` for `text`. To make the clock run, we need only one line of code, but we'll need an event for that, see the *Events and actors*, and *Timer events* sections later.

Using do in view

Inside the `view` code block, ordinary binding statements such as n: 2 ** 3 and `print` n *must* be placed within a `do` block, like this:

```
;-- see Chapter09/container-layout.red:
view [
    text "Use of do block"
    do [n: 2 ** 3 print n]
]
```

A `do` block can be used to evaluate code and initialize or make changes to the GUI, before the layout is displayed.

All other code must appear within action facet code blocks, such as our button-click code [download-rates].

Layout commands

Red works with the normal *coordinate system*, with the origin `0x0` in the top-left corner:

A point with coordinates (*n*, *m*) is noted as `nxm`. Such a `pair!` value can also be used in the `face/offset` property, which describes the position of the top-left corner of the face from the origin, in this case *n* pixels from the left, and *m* pixels down. It can also be used to move a face to a new position:

```
;-- see Chapter09/offset.red:
t: text "I will not stay here"
button "Move text" [t/offset: 20x30]
```

By default, Red uses a kind of flow layout represented with the `across` word. Faces are placed from left to right until the screen line is full, then the line below is filled, and so on.

A number of words besides `across` and `below` exist to fine-tune this process:

- `return` places the next face on a line horizontally below while in `across` mode, or on a line vertically beside it while in `below` mode
- `at nxm` places the next face (and only that) with its top-left corner at an absolute position (*n*, *m*)
- `origin nxm` starts the window layout at position (*n*, *m*) instead of (0, 0)
- `pad wxh`, where *w* is width and *h* is height, specifies that the next face starts *w* pixels to the right and *h* pixels down
- `space wxh`, where *w* is width and *h* is height, specifies the new spacing between the next faces in width and height (in other words, the offset)

To get a feeling for how these commands work, experiment with them in question 4 from the *Questions* section.

A faces walkthrough

The VID dialect contains some 20 different faces (graphical widgets), each with its own specific properties (*facets*). The type of that value specifies what the facet does. For example, a string will be used as the displayed text for the face, or a pair will determine its size. Most faces also have a default *action facet*, that is, a block of commands that is triggered by a certain event, such as clicking on a button or selecting from a list.

We cannot possibly discuss them all in detail, instead we'll do a walkthrough of the kinds of faces that are available, what you can do with them, and highlight some important properties. You're encouraged to try these out (together with the questions), as we go along.

Base, box, and image

We start with the most basic types:

Here is the VID code:

```
;-- see Chapter09/base-box-image.red:
view [
    base
    box red
    image 140x140 %heads.jpg
    below
    text "I am a button:"
    button %heads.jpg [quit]
]
```

`Base` is the most primitive of them all. It displays a gray rectangle, but it can respond to a click (`on-down`) event; it can show an image, and it can be used to draw inside it. A *box* is like a base, but it is transparent by default, so we give it a color to make it show.

An `image` is a base face with a default size of 100 x 100, used to show a picture. Whenever a face has an image file as a facet, it is used as a background image for that face. See the button example. A `camera` facet is also available to capture a video stream when that hardware is available, for example on mobile devices.

Text faces – h1, text, field, and area

Here is a window using text faces:

Here is the code to produce that window (note that in a real app we must give our widgets meaningful names, instead of `t1` and `f1`!):

```
; see Chapter09/text-faces.red:
view [
    title "Text faces"
    below
    h3 "Heading 3"
    t1: text 300x30 bold italic blue font-name "algerian"
        font-color ivory font-size 14 "Text with properties"
    text "Click me!" [face/color: orange face/text: "FIRE!"]
    f1: field 300 "Type something here" [ print [f1/data] ]
    a: area 300x100 [print a/text]
]
```

To show text in a window, use the `text` face. Some basic h1, h2 to h5 text styles for headings are available, as in h3 "Heading 3". Text can be put in bold, italic, underline, or strike mode, and if a color is mentioned, this is used as the background color. For the text font, any font-name your system knows can be used. The font-size and font-color can also be specified.

The color can be specified as a predefined name, such as red, aqua, navy, or orange. But you can also specify a color through its RGB values as a tuple! such as 40.100.130, or 40.100.130.A, where A is the transparency value ranging from 0 to 255. You can get a list of the named colors by typing ? tuple! in the console.

Clicking on some text activates its action facet. As illustrated by the **Click me!** text, a face can be addressed inside its own action block by the face word.

Use a field to get input text from the user and stored in its word f1, more precisely, in its text facet f1/text. An integer specifies the field's length in pixels, a string can be used to display some predefined text if needed. The text inside the field is also contained in the /data property. The default action of a field is triggered by pressing the *Enter* key while in the field. This is the on-enter event. We use that to print out the field's input in the console.

If you need a multiline space for text, use an area. The text inside it is contained in the /text facet of the face. Any keystroke inside the area activates its action block (the on-change event), here again printing to the console.

Because the action code blocks were short, we didn't bother to give them a name. In a real app, where the action code is more than one line, you should put that code in a function (declared before the view), and call that function in the action facet. Such a function can refer to the face and the event that triggered the action by the arguments called face and event. That's what we did in our download exchange rates example with the download-rates function. Separating the GUI from the code logic helps later maintenance of the program.

Button, check, and radio

Here is a window using button faces:

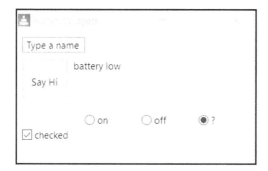

Here is its code:

```
; see Chapter09/button-faces.red:
view [
    title "Button Widgets"
    below
    name: field 100 "Type a name"
    across
    button 70x70 "Say Hi" center [t1/text: append "Hi " name/text]
    t1: text ""
    return
    ch1: check 90x70 "Check me" [
            either ch1/data
                [ch1/text: "checked"]
                [ch1/text: "unchecked"]
    ]
    r1: radio "on"  [t1/text: "too loud!"]
    r2: radio "off" [t1/text: "that's better"]
    r3: radio "?"   [t1/text: "battery low"]
]
```

Buttons are specifically used for the actions they produce when they are clicked. Here we change text content to the input of the name field. The default event is on-click, which for a button is the same as on-down. Notice the center word used to position the text. To do that, you can also use top, middle, bottom, left, right, and combinations.

A checkbox is a `check` face, typically used for asking yes or no questions. It has optional text, `/text`. Its value is contained in its `/data` property, and it can be true (checkbox checked) or false (not checked). However, `check` has a default `on-change` event, here we use it to show the status of the checkbox.

The radio button is a `radio` face with exactly the same properties as `check`. Use it when the user has to choose one (and only one) out of more than two possibilities.

=> Now solve question 5 from the *Questions* section.

List faces – text-list, drop-list, and drop-down

Often a data item can take any of a discrete number of values stored in a series. For this, we need to use some kind of list face. Here is a window using list faces, from left to right, `text-list`, `drop-list`, and `drop-down`:

Here is the code:

```
;-- see Chapter09/list-faces.red:
city-trip: copy ["Paris" "London" "Leipzig" "Rome" "New York" "Beijing"]
view [
    title "List faces"
    t1: text "Click on a city to visit ->"
    text-list 100x100 data city-trip [t1/text: pick face/data
face/selected]
    t2: text "Click on a city to visit ->"
    drop-list data city-trip [t2/text: pick face/data face/selected]
    t3: text "Click on a city to visit ->"
    drop-down data city-trip [t3/text: pick face/data face/selected print
t3/text]
    ;               on-change [t3/text: pick face/data face/selected print
t3/text]
]
```

To show strings in list form, use the `text-list` face. Here, we display a list of cities through the `data` property of the `text-list`. Selecting an item from the list (the `on-select` event) is done with the code `pick face/data face/selected`. This works because `face/selected` is the index of the selected item, and `face/data` is a series. Notice that the scroll bars appear automatically when needed.

A `drop-list` shows the values in a collapsed list. Click on the down-arrow to see the data items. Selecting an item triggers the `on-change` event.

A `drop-down` also works the same, but its default event is `on-enter`, so you have to select a value with the up and down arrows, and then press *ENTER*. If you want it to work like the other two lists, you have to say which event you mean, like this, `on-change` `[t3/text: pick face/data face/selected]`.

(To see this, add a `print` statement like `print t3/text` which prints its result to the console.)

You can also type in the textbox at the top, which goes into the `/text` property.

=> Now solve questions 6 and 7 from the *Questions* section.

Panel, group-box, and tab-panel

To divide your app screen surface into distinct areas, you can use group-boxes, panels, or tab-panels. Here is an example showing all of them:

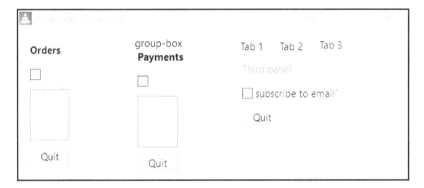

Here is the code:

```
;-- see Chapter09/panels.red:
view [
    panel yellow bold [ size 150x200 below
                        text bold "Orders"
                        check
                        area 60x75
                        button "Quit" [quit]
    ]
    group-box green "group-box" bold
                    [ size 150x200 below
                        text bold "Payments"
                        check
                        area 60x75
                        button "Quit" [quit]
    ]
    tbp: tab-panel 250x150 [
        "Tab 1" [h4 "In panel 1!" button "Click in 1" [print tbp/data] ]
        "Tab 2" [text "Second panel" button "Click in 2" [print tbp/pane]
    ]
        "Tab 3" [below text font-color red "Third panel"
                check "subscribe to email?"
                button "Quit" [print tbp/selected quit]
        ]
    ]
]
```

A panel and a group-box are very similar and serve only to contain other related faces in a rectangular area. They can't respond to events on their own, but the faces they contain can. A group-box has a visible frame with optional text. You can use as many of them as you need.

A tab-panel really divides a screen into sub-screens, but only one of them is visible at a time; the other sub-screens can be reached by clicking on their tab heading. Some useful details are as follows:

- /data gives a block with the tab names, here—Tab 1, Tab 2, and Tab 3
- /pane gives a list of the panels with their properties
- /selected gives the index of the selected tab (1 for Tab 1 and so on)

We'll use panels in our contacts app.

Progress bar and slider

As their names suggest, these faces exist to indicate the increase or decrease of a certain quantity. A progress bar is passive, only displaying the status. A slider can be moved to indicate progress or a decrease, which is an on-change event. Both faces keep the quantity in /data as a percent! value (such as 25 %). If you specify it as a float between 0.0 and 1.0, you will need to convert this value with to-percent.

Here are some examples of their use:

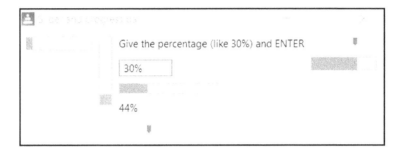

Here is the code to do that:

```
;-- see Chapter09/progress-slider.red:
view [
    across
    p1: progress 100x20 10%      ;-- horizontal progress bar:
    p2: progress 20x100 15%      ;-- vertical progress bar:
    ;-- bar following input:
    below
    text "Give the percentage (like 30%) and ENTER"
    field [p3/data: face/data]
    p3: progress
    ;-- slider showing status in text:
    t: text "25%"
    slider 100x20 data 25% [t/text: to-string face/data]
    return
    ;-- slider displayed in a progress bar:
    slider 100x20 data 10% [p4/data: face/data]
    p4: progress 100x20 10%
]
```

Progress bars can also be used vertically as you can see. In the third one, the progress is kept in sync with a field's input. A slider has a default *change* event when it is moved; here it shows its status in a text field. In the rightmost example, this event keeps a progress bar synchronized with the slider.

Styles

If your app needs several instances of a face with the same properties and actors, for example, the tiles for a board game or the buttons of a calculator, you can define that as a style with a name and use that name instead. This is illustrated in the following tile game (in 10 lines!) from Nick Antoniacci:

```
;-- see Chapter09/tile.red:
view [
    title "Tile Game"
    backdrop silver
    style t1: button 100x100 [
        temp: face/offset
        face/offset: empty/offset
        empty/offset: temp
    ]
    t1 "8" t1 "7" t1 "6" return
    t1 "5" t1 "4" t1 "3" return
    t1 "2" t1 "1" empty: base silver
]
```

We defined a style t1 for all eight buttons we need. Clicking on a tile button moves that button to the empty space, empty, by setting its offset to the offset of empty. Then empty moves to the tile's place by setting its offset to temp, which is the button's offset. It looks like this:

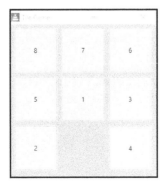

So, `style` is used to make customized faces, and the properties of `style` can be overridden in the concrete widgets.

Events and actors

In the previous examples, we saw that most faces can have actors, which are event handlers that execute when a certain event occurs on that face. For example, the slider in the code we just explored has a default *on-change* actor, which is the code in the last block:

```
slider 100x20 data 25% [t/text: to-string face/data]
```

Not all faces can respond to all sorts of events. But a lot of faces can respond to multiple events as well.

Red defines some 40 events for which you can define actors on your faces. You can find the complete list here: `https://doc.red-lang.org/en/view.html#_events`.

Actors all have short names, such as *move*, *over*, or *down*. If we break them down into categories, we can distinguish the following:

- *mouse events*, such as `down`, `up`, `drag`, `drop`, `click`, `dbl-click`, `over`, `wheel`, and so on, including events for all three buttons, the mouse wheel, and hovering over faces
- *window events*, such as `move` and `resize`
- *keyboard events*, such as `key`, `key-down`, `key-up`, and `enter`
- *touch events*, such as `zoom`, `pan`, `rotate`, and `tapping`
- a *timer event* (`time`)
- *general events*, such as `focus`, `select`, `change`, and `menu`

To implement an actor on a face, specify an *on-event* name before its code block. This is only necessary for additional actors, not for the default actor. In the following sections, we look at some typical examples and learn more about their internals.

Multiple events

Implementing multiple events is easy. Here is an example where four actors are defined for a button:

```
;-- see Chapter09/multiple-events.red:
view [
    below
    message: text 100x25 green "Nothing"
    button "Different things happen"
        [message/text: "A click!"]                    ; default event
        on-over [message/text: "Hovering!"]   ; hovering cursor over face
        on-dbl-click [message/text: "A double click!"]
        on-wheel [message/text: "Wheeling!"]      ; turning mouse wheel
]
```

This is displayed as follows:

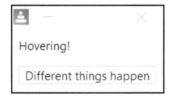

 Note that a left mouse button click is called `on-click` only for button widgets, for all other faces it is an `on-down`, followed by an `on-up` event.

=> Now answer question 8 from the *Questions* section.

Timer event

For this kind of event, there is an `on-time` actor. This actor works together with the face's `rate` facet, which sets the rate at which the event takes place, either expressed in:

- Rate per second, such as one time per second: `rate 1`, so rate 50 is 50 times faster than rate 1
- As a `time!` value, such as rate 0:00:03 for every 3 seconds

At each tick, the `on-time` actor is executed. Here are a few simple examples. Note how we can achieve some primitive animation effects by changing the `offset` in an `on-time` actor:

```
;-- see Chapter09/timers.red:
view [
    size 400x400
    b: button 80x30 green "Catch me" rate 50
        on-time [b/offset: b/offset + 1x1]
        on-down [quit]
    t1: text txt rate 5
        on-time [either t1/text = "" [t1/text: txt][t1/text: ""]]
    t2: text txt rate 0:00:03
        on-time [either t2/text = "" [t2/text: txt][t2/text: ""]]
]
```

Now it's time to make our digital clock from the *Container settings* section work. To do that, we only need to add one line (shown in bold) that defines the `on-time` actor, which executes every second:

```
;-- see Chapter09/digital-clock2.red:
time-now: to string! now/time
view/flags [
    title "Clock"
    show-time: text font-size 13 font-color red time-now
    rate 1 on-time [show-time/text: to string! now/time]
]
[modal popup]
```

Actors are objects

If you have solved question 2, you will know that a face is a complex object with many facets. The actor(s) it contains are stored in one facet, which is an object with one field per event. Suppose we have the following code for a button:

```
;-- see Chapter09/faces-are-objects.red:
bt: button "Print me!" [print bt]
```

Click the button and then scroll down to the end of the console output, you will find the following:

```
actors: make object! [
    on-click: func [face [object!] event [event! none!]][print bt]
]
```

We'll apply it in the following two sections.

Detecting the keyboard

An actor is in fact a combination of an event name and a function that takes some arguments, principally the widget on which the event occurs and the event itself. The following code snippet shows how to detect when certain keys are pressed:

```
;-- see Chapter09/key-detecting.red:
view/options [
    t: text "hit 'space', 'a', or '?' keys !"][
    actors: object [on-key: func [key event] [
            if event/key = #"a" [t/text: "'a' key pressed."]
            if event/key = #"?" [t/text: "'?' key pressed."]
            if event/key = #" " [t/text: "'space bar'pressed."]
        ]
    ]
]
```

Menus

The fact that actors are objects becomes very much apparent when we see how menu events are defined in Red. The definition of a menu starts by declaring a `layout` object. Then, via a `/menu` field, the menu titles and submenus are defined as a list. Each submenu is a deeper nested level in the list, for example:

```
; see Chapter09/menu.red:
mex: layout [title "Menu example" ar: area cyan 400x400]
mex/menu: [
    "File" [ "Load" load --- "Save" sv --- "Save As" svas --- "Print" prnt
]
    "Sub-menus" [
        "Submenu1" s1
        "Submenu2" s2
        "Submenu3" [
            "Submenu4" s4
            "Submenu5" s5
        ]
    ]
    "Tools" [ "Text Size" txts ]
    "Help" [ "Some Help" hlp ]
    "Quit" [ "Close all" qt]
]
```

Each menu item has a title as a string and a word, which stores the event that occurs when this menu item is clicked. For example, "`Close all`" and `qt` for the **Quit** menu.

Then, we define the menu actors with `/actors` as an object that contains the `on-menu` actor, which is a function with `face` and `event` arguments. The word corresponding to the event that fired sits in `event/picked`, so we can use a simple `if`, or a `switch` if there are many menus, to attach the respective code block:

```
mex/actors: make object! [
    on-menu: func [face [object!] event [event!]][
        switch event/picked [
            load [print "load" ar/text: "Load !"]
            sv [print "save" ar/text: "Save !"]
            svas [print "save as" ar/text: "Save As !"]
            s4 [print "submenu4 selected" ar/text: "Submenu 4"]
            txts [print "Tools tab !" ar/text: "Tools tab !"]
            hlp [print "help tab !" ar/text: "Help tab !"]
            prnt [print "print menu selected" ar/text: "Print tab !"]
            qt [quit]
        ]
    ]
]

view mex
```

Basic contacts app

Let's now combine some of the things we have learned so far and start building a maintenance app for the contacts we used throughout Chapters 5, *Working with Series and Blocks*, and Chapter 7, *Working with Files*. Our data store is a text file named `contacts`. Each line has the contact's name, the contact's address, and a telephone number, all fields separated by a semicolon (;).

Here's an example:

```
John Smith;123 Tomline Lane Forest Hills, NJ;555-1234
Paul Thompson;234 Georgetown Pl. Grove, AL;555-2345
```

Here is the application screen:

The names of our contacts are shown in the `text-list` face. When a name is selected, this contact's details appear in the fields in the panel on the right. A new contact can be filled in and added to the list. When the **Save** button is pressed, all contacts are saved to the `contacts` file.

Here is the code. By now, you should understand what is happening, but we have added some remarks to help you if needed:

```
;-- see Chapter09/contacts-app.red:
extract-info: func [] [
    clear names
    clear addresses
    clear phones
    foreach contact contacts [
        arr-contact: split contact ";"
        append names arr-contact/1
        append addresses arr-contact/2
        append phones arr-contact/3
    ]
]

clear-fields: func [] [
    name/text: copy ""                              ; (1)
    address/text: copy ""
    phone/text: copy ""
]
```

```
if not find read %. %contacts [write %contacts ""]        ; (2)
contacts: read/lines %contacts                            ; (3)
names: copy []                                            ; (4)
addresses: copy []
phones: copy []
extract-info                                              ; (5)
view [
    title "Contacts"
    tl: text-list data names [
        name/text: pick tl/data tl/selected              ; (6)
        address/text: pick addresses tl/selected
        phone/text: pick phones tl/selected
    ]
    panel [
        below
        text "Name:"
        name: field 200
        text "Address:"
        address: field 250
        text "Phone:"
        phone: field 100
        button "Add" [                                    ; (7)
            new-contact: rejoin [ name/text ";" address/text ";"
phone/text]
            append contacts new-contact                   ; (8)
            clear-fields
            extract-info
        ]
        button "Save" [
            write/lines %contacts contacts                ; (9)
            clear-fields
        ]
        button "Clear" [clear-fields]
    ]
]
```

Let's see what some of the code lines do:

1. We use `copy` here, see `Chapter 5`, *Working with Series and Blocks*.
2. See if there is already a contacts' file in the current directory (`%.`), if not, create an empty one.
3. `read/lines` reads in the `contacts` file as a block of strings, each string is one contact (to see this, insert a `probe contacts`).

4. This declaration is needed, because the word `names` already appears in the function `extract-names`; `names` must be declared before `extract-names` is called. Again, we use `copy` here, see `Chapter 5`, *Working with Series and Blocks*.

5. In the `extract-info` function, which is called here, we extract the name, address, and phone info in three separate lists, but the info of each contact has the same index in each list.

6. For that reason we can use the same index `tl/selected` here, to show each data item in its appropriate field.

7. In the following line we create a string with the new contact info.

8. The new contact string is appended to the `contacts` series.

9. The new `contacts` series is written out to the `contacts` file, each contact on a separate line.

An introduction to the draw dialect

Draw is a Red dialect created to make it easy to draw two-dimensional geometrical shapes such as circles, rectangles, and animations. It makes use of VID, so the `needs 'view` has to appear in the header. To start with a simple example, here is how to draw a circle:

```
;-- see Chapter09/first-draw-example.red:
view [
    base 100x100 cyan draw [
        line 20x0 75x50
        pen red
        circle 35x50 20
    ]
]
```

We draw on a `base` face and start a `draw` block. In it, we draw a `line` from a starting point at 20 x 0 to an end point at 75 x 50. Then, we define a `pen` with the color red and use it to draw a `circle` with a radius of 20 and center at 35 x 50:

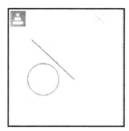

=> Now answer question 9 from the *Questions* section.

Instead of a `base`, you can also add drawings on an existing `image`.

The draw dialect is very elaborate, here are some of the things you can try out:

- Draw rectangles (`box`), triangles, polygons, ellipses, curves, arcs, special fonts, and so on
- Set the `line-width` of the pen to draw thicker lines (for example, `line-width 10`)
- Fill up shapes by setting `fill-pen` with a color (for example, `fill-pen yellow`)
- If you don't need borders set, type `pen off`
- Text can be drawn at a specific point, such as `text 40x30`
- Different kinds of gradients can be used with `pen` and `fill-pen`
- You can use transformations, such as translation, scaling, and rotation
- By combining `draw` with `on-time` actors, animations can be run

In the *Reactive programming* section in `Chapter 10`, *Advanced Red*, we will show some really cool examples of what can be done when all these functionalities are combined.

Consult the links on draw in the *Further reading* section if you want to go really indepth.

Summary

In this chapter, you got an overview of the VID dialect for making graphical applications. First, we made a VID version of our download exchange rate app, to see how to use different faces in the `view` block. We discussed the different `options` for view for making special windows, and the `layout` commands such as `below`, `return`, and `at` to structure your screens.

Then, we guided you through a tour of the faces available, such as `text`, `field`, `button`, `check`, `drop-list`, `panel`, `tab-panel`, `slider`, `menus`, and so on. To really build dynamic screens, you have to use `actors` on these different faces. You learned how to code them, combine multiple actors on one face, detect keys, and make timed events. We also gave an example of how you can start building more complicated maintenance apps. Finally, you got an introduction to the very powerful draw dialect, which enables you to draw 2D shapes and animations.

Questions

1. Rewrite `download-rates` in `currency-rates-gui.red` so that it accepts the code and date as parameters.
2. Print out the internal structure of a `button` object to the Red console. Notice that `button` has a `window` parent face.
3. You can code a button to close its window by using the `quit` or the `unview` word in its action facet. Try both out. Note that `unview/all` is used when there are multiple windows to close.
4. Create a window that displays square `base` faces with different colors, such as `base yellow 25x25`. Try out several of the layout commands.
5. Make a window with a button and a checkbox. Change the state and text of the checkbox with a click on the button. After three clicks, disable that button (hint: use `face/enabled?` for that).
6. Make a window that displays the data values of a series sorted in a text-list. You can do this in two ways—with a button action, or with a `do` block.
7. Extract the names from the series `["Dave" 1804 "Peter" 9439 "Viviane" 2386 "Marcus" 9423]` and show them in a `text-list`. When a name is selected, show the corresponding number in a `text` field. Also, print out the index of that name in the original list to the console.
8. Create a window displaying text that changes its background color when the mouse cursor hovers over it. Also define a list of strings, for example, cities. Define an on-wheel actor that displays each of the cities in turn.
9. On a rectangular base of width 500 and height 300 with white background, draw red diagonals in the rectangle and blue perpendicular lines.

Further reading

You can find some additional information about VID here: `http://www.red-by-example.org/vid.html`.

Much more info about the drawing dialect can be found here: `http://www.red-by-example.org/draw.html`.

Official docs about the GUI system are, for the time being, rather formal and can be found here: `https://doc.red-lang.org/en/gui.html`. It includes in-depth info about the View engine, VID, and the draw dialect.

10
Advanced Red

In this final chapter, we will explore some more advanced aspects of the language, and will look at where Red is heading in the near future. Reactive programming is a great way to write more responsive (GUI) apps. We encountered Red/System as the lower-level foundation of Red in Chapter 1, *Red's Mission*, and Chapter 2, *Setting Up for Development*. Here, we'll see how you can use it, either in Red apps, or standalone.

The following topics will be covered in this chapter:

- Reactive programming
- Red/System
- Interacting with the operating system
- Datatypes for performance
- Embedded Red and macros
- Red for smart contract programming
- Red's roadmap
- Some useful references

Technical requirements

You'll find the code for this chapter at https://github.com/PacktPublishing/Learn-Red-Fundamentals-of-Red/tree/master/Chapter10. If you have installed Red as indicated in Chapter 2, *Setting Up for Development*, you are good to go. You can work on Windows, OS X, or Linux. You can type or paste any code in the Red console to see its results, or you can start using an editor such as Visual Studio Code.

Reactive programming

In Chapter 9, *Composing Visual Interfaces*, we saw how easy it is to handle events on widgets by attaching actor code blocks. We encountered several examples where a change or action in one face influenced another face—for example, clicking a button changes a text in a field. The text field reacted to the button because we explicitly coded an actor on the button.

Look at the following code snippet:

```
;-- see Chapter10/reactive1.red:
point: [x: 3 y: 5]
distance: square-root (point/x ** 2) + (point/y ** 2)
print distance      ;== 5.8309518948453
point/x: 2
print distance      ;== 5.8309518948453      <-- doesn't change!
distance: square-root (point/x ** 2) + (point/y ** 2)
print distance      ;== 5.385164807134504  <-- changed
```

The distance word gives the distance of point to the origin, but when the point's coordinates change, distance does not change automatically with it. Only when distance is asked to calculate itself again after the change do we get an updated result.

You can imagine that it would be useful to have words update their values automatically when a change occurs—for example, when keeping track of a running total, or a calculation in a spreadsheet cell. Red has built this into its reactive framework. Here's how you can use it to make distance follow changes in point:

```
point: make reactor! [x: 3 y: 5]
distance: is [square-root (point/x ** 2) + (point/y ** 2)]
print distance      ;== 5.8309518948453
point/x: 2
print distance      ;== 5.385164807134504
```

The point word is a so-called **reactor**, the cause or *source* of a change; this is indicated with make reactor!. Changes in the fields of the reactor *automatically* (that is, without calling a function) trigger changes in other *target* objects, such as distance in this example. These target(s) are defined as a **reactive expression** by using the is [ ] word. Changes are propagated from source to target:

reactor (source) ----> target(s).

A reactor can even update itself, which takes less code, as we can see here:

```
point: make reactor! [
    x: 3
    y: 5
    distance: is [square-root (x ** 2) + (y ** 2)]
]
point ;== make object! [x: 3 y: 5 distance: 5.8309518948453]
point/x: 2
point ;== make object! [x: 2 y: 5 distance: 5.385164807134504]
```

Don't let the change cause a change in itself, provoking an endless loop!

The source of the change must be an object with fields, such as `point/x` and `point/y` in the example. If the target refers to more than one nested level (such as `shape/point/x`), use `make deep-reactor!` instead of `make-reactor!`.

This reactivity can also be used when writing graphical interfaces—instead of coding an actor, use the `react` word on the target side. The following example compares the synchronization between a slider and a progress bar done in two ways. In `Tab 1`, reactive programming is used (the progress bar is the target), and, in `Tab 2`, we take the actor code from the previous chapter:

```
;-- see Chapter10/reactive-gui.red
view [
    origin 0x0 space 0x0
    tab-panel 500x500 [
        "Tab 1 " [
            progress 100x20 data 20% react [face/data: s/data]
            s: slider 100x20 data 20%
        ]
        "Tab 2 " [
            p: progress 100x20 20%
            slider 100x20 data 20% [p/data: face/data]
        ]
    ]
]
```

The reactive framework is only some 250 lines of Red code and is quite versatile. An object can be the target of many source objects, and you can create chains of reacting objects as well. This framework doesn't let you do things you couldn't do before, but it makes you think in another way about problems, and your code will be more compact, readable, and declarative.

For an impressive demo of a clock combining `draw` , `react`, and live coding, see `https://www.red-lang.org/2016/07/eve-style-clock-demo-in-red-livecoded.html`.

=> Now solve questions 1 and 2 from the *Questions* section.

Red/System

Red/System, the C-level, purely imperative dialect of Red, has four main purposes:

- It has the role of an **IR (intermediate representation)** language for compiled Red code, and efficiently compiles directly into machine code for all targets, so it does not generate C or assembler as an intermediary.
- It is the language in which part of Red itself and notably the *runtime system* is written.
- It can be embedded inside Red apps for fast code support, so, whenever your Red app needs to run faster, you can rewrite the code pieces that perform the worst in Red/System to achieve huge performance gains.
- It can be used to write *low-level programs* and perform *system programming*.

 Red/System is a dialect, a subset of Red, and an embedded **DSL (domain-specific language)** of its host language Red, yet the host is implemented in that dialect.

You can find the Red/System source code in the `red-source/runtime` and `red-source/system/runtime` folders.

Comparing Red and Red/System

There are very good reasons to get to know Red/System better. It will look familiar to you because it uses the same syntax structures as Red, so you will not have to change mental gears when stepping from Red to Red/System and vice versa. In fact, some small code snippets may be completely identical, as the following Red/System script shows:

```
;-- see Chapter10/hello-world.reds:
Red/System [
    Title: "Hello World demo"
]
print "Hello world from Red/System!"
```

Looks very much like Red, doesn't it? The only differences are the `Red/System [ ]` header and the `.reds` file extension.

Also, the Red/System code can't be interpreted; you have to compile it using `red -r hello-world.reds`, which works lightning fast.

Let's compare a function for calculating factorials (see the *Recursive functions* section in Chapter 6, *Using Functions and Objects*). Remember that, in Red, the following did the trick:

```
fact: func [n][
    if n = 0 [ return 1]
    n * fact n - 1
]
```

In Red/System, this becomes the following:

```
;-- see Chapter10/fact.reds:
fact: func [
    n [integer!]
    return: [integer!]
][
    if n = 0 [ return 1]
    n * fact n - 1
]
```

Note that the calculation code stays the same, but that in Red/System, *function argument typing and the declaration of the return value with* `return:` *are mandatory*.

To better appreciate the difference, here is a comparison between a `as-color` function that takes three integers `r`, `g`, and `b`, and returns them as a tuple. Here is the Red version:

```
;-- see Chapter10/as-color.red:
as-color: function [
    r [integer!]
    g [integer!]
    b [integer!]
][
    make tuple! reduce [r g b]
]
print as-color 153 255 51 ;== 153.255.51
```

Compare this with the Red/System version:

```
as-color: function [
    r [integer!]
    g [integer!]
    b [integer!]
    /local arr1 [integer!]
][
    arr1: (b % 256 << 16) or (g % 256 << 8) or (r % 256)
    stack/set-last as red-value! tuple/push 3 arr1 0 0
]
```

You can see that the last version uses bitwise manipulations, and the result has to be written to a stack.

Red/System provides support for low-level CPU register operations (interruptions, I/O, stack, privileged mode) and for an inlined assembler. It has to use values that can fit into CPU/FPU registers, and gives you complete control over memory allocation.

Compared to Red, its host language, it has only a few primitive types, such as `logic!`, `byte!`, `integer!`, `float!`, `float32!`, `function!`, `c-string!`, `struct!`, and `pointer!`.

A `c-string!` type facilitates the interaction with C libraries, while `struct!` and `pointer!` make precise control over memory allocation and access possible.

Calling a Red/System script from within Red

To delegate high-performance code snippets to Red/System, we need a way to call into Red/System from Red. Suppose we want to call our Red/System `fact` function from a Red script. This is done as follows:

```
;-- see Chapter10/use-fact.red:
#system-global [#include %fact.reds]          ; (1)

red-fact: routine [                           ; (2)
    n [integer!]                              ; (3)
    return: [integer!]
][
    fact n  ; function from fact.reds         ; (4)
]

print red-fact 9 ;== 362880                   ; (5)
```

In line `(1)`, the Red/System script is included as usual Red scripts, but it must be prefixed by `#system-global`, a *directive*. This line also executes the Red/System script, so be sure to remove or comment out any executable code from it. As indicated in line `(2)`, a Red function that calls a Red/System function is of the special `routine!` type. Line `(3)` and the line following it tell us that a routine must type its arguments and return a value. In line `(4)`, the Red/System function is referenced, while in line `(5)`, the `fact` function is actually called.

Red/System code can contain other compiler directives as well, such as `#define`, `#include`, `#import`, `#syscall`, `#if`, `#either`, `#switch`, and so on. They form a part of a *preprocessor* dialect, which can also be used in Red itself. You can find more information about the preprocessor at `https://doc.red-lang.org/en/preprocessor.html`.

A Red program that includes Red/System code must be compiled in release mode as `red -r use-fact.red`; the included Red/System script doesn't need to be compiled beforehand.

The `do` word does not work here because it only interprets the code.

=> Now answer questions 3 and 4 from the *Questions* section.

Just for fun, you can see the Red/System generated code from compiling the Red source when you add a `-v` flag to the compilation command, as in `red -r **-v 3** hello-world.red > output` (open the `output` file in any text editor).

Interacting with the operating system

Some of the things you must be able to do when writing apps include getting information at startup, starting up a different program from within your app, and using the OS clipboard. Here, we'll show you how this is done in Red.

Getting input from command-line arguments

Command-line arguments are captured in the `system/script/args` word. It is one string in which all arguments are stored, separated by a space:

```
;-- see Chapter10/args.red:
print system/script/args          ;== "78 A Red"
type? system/script/args          ;== string!
args: split system/script/args " " ;== ["78" "A" "Red"]
print ["Number of command-line arguments:" length? args]
```

```
                                             ;== Number of command-line arguments: 3
foreach arg args [
    print arg
]
; 78
; A
; Red
```

We can use `split` to obtain the separated arguments in an `args` series, and start using them.

To see the output, start the program with `red args.red 78 A Red`, or after compiling with `red -r`, start it with: `./args 78 A Red`.

Calling an external program – call

Running an external process, program, or shell script from within a Red app is easy—just use the `call` word. Here are some examples you can try out in the Red console:

```
;-- see Chapter10/interacting-os.red:
call "explorer.exe" ;== 9668 (1)
call/shell "notepad.exe" ;== 2292 (2)
call/shell "notepad.exe info.txt" ;== 11632 (3)
cmd: "notepad.exe info.txt"
call/shell cmd ;== 7244 (4)
call/shell/wait "notepad.exe" ;== 0 (5)
call/output "ls" %listing ;== 0 (6)
call "start copy nul > myfile.txt" ;== 13760 (7)
```

Let's break down what's happening line by line:

1. Here, we start Windows Explorer.
2. Notepad is started (on Windows).
3. Here, a file `info.txt` will be opened in Notepad.
4. You can store the `shell` command in a word.
5. In the previous cases, the Red app continues. If you want it to wait until the started process has finished, use `/wait`.
6. Write the output of the command to the given file (here, this is on Linux/OS X). The output could also be a variable.
7. Any valid `shell` command can be given to `call`. Here, we use `start` on Windows to create an empty file.

The `call` value returned is either the process-id of the started program, or else 0 when the startup is successful, and –1 when an error occurs.

Using the OS clipboard – read-clipboard

The following code temporarily stores some information to the clipboard:

```
write-clipboard "Some important info" ;== true
; close Red console or Red program
print read-clipboard ;== Some important info
```

This can be used as a means of communication between two Red apps. The info stays on the clipboard until the OS restarts or until another program writes to the clipboard.

Datatypes for performance

We all love and know our trusted series, but certain apps need all the performance they can get, especially when dealing with large datasets. For that specific reason, the `vector!`, `map!`, and `hash!` datatypes were constructed.

The vector! datatype

When your series contains values of one of the `integer!`,`float!`, `char!`, or `percent!` types and only one of these, and you need fast mathematical operations, then you want to use the `vector!` type, like this:

```
;-- see Chapter10/perf-datatypes.red:
v1: make vector! [7 13 42 108]
vector? v1        ;== true
```

In a `vector!`, all values need to be of the same type. You can perform simple arithmetic with vectors like so:

```
v1 + 2          ;== make vector! [9 15 44 110]
print v1        ;== 9 15 44 110
v1 * 4          ;== make vector! [36 60 176 440]
v2: make vector! [1 2 3 4]
v1 + v2         ;== make vector! [37 62 179 444]
```

Note that the operations on one vector change it in place, that means the vector `v1` in our examples is changed by the operations. Most actions that we know from series can be used with vectors. Here is an example:

```
v1: make vector! [7 13 42 108]
length? v1 ;== 4
append v1 666 ;== make vector! [7 13 42 108 666]
find v1 42 ;== make vector! [42 108 666]
; looping through a vector:
foreach n v1 [prin [n "-"]] ;==7 - 13 - 42 - 108 - 666 -
v1/3 ;== 42
```

The map! and hash! datatypes

Many languages have a dictionary type to efficiently store values associated with keys, and to provide fast lookup for those keys—for example, key1 -> value1, key2 -> value2, and so on. Red offers two datatypes for this, the `hash!` and the `map!`.

With `hash!`, you get a type that has all the navigational functionality that exists for series. When the key values are simple types, they get hashed, which results in a *fast value lookup*. First, you define the key, then its value, then a new key with its value, and so on:

```
h1: make hash! [n 13 m 42 o 108]
h1/m            ;== 42
select h1 [m]   ;== 42
select h1 'm    ;== 42

hash? h1        ;== true
hash? [n 13 m 42 o 108]    ;== false
```

Value lookup is done with the path notation hash / key or through `select`, with the key represented either in a block or as a literal word. This datatype is especially suited for dealing with large datasets in which you have to constantly search. The `hash!` word can also be used without any key-values, just to provide a series with fast lookup, like this:

```
fruits: ["apple" "ananas" "tomato" "strawberry" "grap"]
to-hash fruits  ;== make hash! ["apple" "ananas" "tomato" "strawberry"
"grap"]
pick fruits 3   ;== "tomato"
```

The map! type is the preferred type for a high-performance dictionary using a hash table, but in contrast to hash!, it's not of the series! type, so, for example, it doesn't know about index position or offset:

```
m1: make map! ["Red" 1 "Crystal" 7 "Python" 13 "Ruby" 42]
== #(
  "Red" 1
  "Crystal" 7
  "Python" 13
  "Ruby" 42
)
```

However, we can see that it has a convenient special syntax, which can also be used to create a map:

```
m5: #(
    "Red" 1
    "Crystal" 7
)
type? m5 ;== map!
```

To get a value from a map, use select. To insert a new value or modify an existing value, use put. To delete a key-value pair from the map, use put key none:

```
select m1 "Crystal"    ;== 7
put m1 "Crystal" 5     ;== 5
put m1 "Java" 132      ;== 132
put m1 "Ruby" none     ;== none ; delete key "Ruby" and its value
print m1
; output:
"Red" 1
"Crystal" 5
"Python" 13
"Java" 132
```

Use find to check whether a map contains a certain key. If it does, it returns true; otherwise, it returns none. The length? word returns the number of key-value pairs. Use keys-of and values-of to get respectively the keys and values of a map in a block form:

```
find m1 "Crystal" ;== true
find m1 "C#"       ;== none
length? m1         ;== 4
keys-of m1         ;== ["Red" "Crystal" "Python" "Java"]
values-of m1       ;== [1 5 13 132]
body-of m1         ;== ["Red" 1 "Crystal" 5 "Python" 13 "Java" 132]
```

All this functionality makes `map!` the type you should choose to build a dictionary data structure with.

Keys can be of the `any-word!`, `any-string!`, `scalar!`, and `binary!` datatypes.

When the keys are words, the familiar / path notation can be used to retrieve and set values:

```
m4: make map! [n 13 m 42 o 108]
m4/m  ;== 42
m4/m:  43
print m4
; output:
n:  13
m:  43
o:  108
```

When the keys are of another type, the key value has to be enclosed in ( ) in order for the path notation to work. A series of key-value pairs can also be merged with an existing map by using the `extend` word:

```
extend m4 [p 113 q 666]
print m4
;== #(
    n:  13
    m:  43
    o:  108
    p:  113
    q:  666
)
```

The same word can also be used to extend an object with new properties and values.

By default, lookup and modification is case-insensitive—that is, the keys Red, red, and RED are considered the same. If you want to work in a case-sensitive way, use `put/case` and `select/case`.

One of the predefined maps is `list-env`, which gives you a map of OS environment variables (for the current process). You can read out the values of these variables as follows:

```
select list-env "windir"   ;== "C:\WINDOWS" ; on Windows
select list-env "SHELL"    ;== "/bin/bash"
```

=> Try this out in question 5 from the *Questions* section.

Embedded Red and macros

In this short section, we will touch on some advanced topics in Red that you should know about. We'll give you references to more detailed descriptions in case you need them for your projects.

Embedded Red

Software written in languages other than Red can interact with Red through *libRed*, a special version of the Red interpreter and runtime library. That way, for example, a C program can interact with a Red environment. Bindings also exist for Visual Basic, Ruby, and Julia (`https://github.com/joa-quim/Red.jl`). Detailed docs are at `https://doc.red-lang.org/en/libred.html` and `https://github.com/red/red/wiki/libRed for additional examples.`

Macros

Another feature many modern programming languages have is macros. Macros are about transforming code at runtime. By now, you should be convinced that Red is already well equipped to do that with minimal effort; think about all you can do with `do`, `reduce`, and `load`. After all, code is data and data is code! Because Red is first of all a compiled language, macros in Red are more oriented towards transforming code at compile time, but they work equally well when interpreted. Here is an example of a macro to give you a taste:

```
;-- see Chapter10/macros.red:
#macro as-KB: func [n][n * 1024]

print as-KB 64 ;== 65536
```

When the macro is expanded by the preprocessor, the code will result in `print 65536`. This example is a *named macro*, and it acts like a function.

Macros in Red/System are quite different. The preprocessor directives we mentioned briefly in the section on Red/System also allow you to process code while compiling.

You can find more information on macros at `https://www.red-lang.org/2016/12/entering-world-of-macros.html`.

Red for smart contract programming

Although it is a very hyped nowadays, it is widely accepted that the introduction of *blockchain technologies* will have a dramatic impact on many industries and commercial activities, mainly because they are based on a trustworthy, decentralized model of storing transactions. That storage is programmable with *smart contracts*, making it truly adaptable to a multitude of needs. Also running on this blockchain infrastructure are opensource **decentralized applications** (or **dapps**), currently developed in a web stack model. Most of the current technology for developing smart contracts and dapps is web based, and overly complex and bloated. The main language for development on the Ethereum blockchain is Solidity, a language derived from JavaScript, which is known for its design flaws and security shortcomings.

As we mentioned in `Chapter 1`, *Red's Mission*, in Jan 2018, the Red team embarked on a mission to provide a superior solution to smart contract and dapp development based on the innovative Red full stack language and toolchain.

Red/C3

Throughout this book, we have seen that Red, thanks to its metaprogramming capabilities, is especially well suited for creating **domain-specific languages** (**DSLs**). Red already uses a number of dialects, such as parse, vid, draw, and Red/System. The Red team is building a DSL for smart contract and dapp programming, called **Red Cross Chain Code** (**Red/C3**). This dialect will compile directly to the bytecode of the different **virtual machines** (**VM**) of the blockchains it will target; it will first run on the Ethereum framework. The dapps' user interfaces will be built with Red's cross-platform GUI capabilities we discussed in the previous chapter.

Red/C3, written in Red, will consist of two layers:

- *A very high-level layer* of specialized, almost natural language that is a restricted subset to provide higher safety. This layer can call into the lower, general purpose layer.
- *A lower general-purpose layer*, a statically typed subset of Red for general computational work.

They will be able to call contracts written in other languages for external compatibility. The first alpha of the Red/C3 compiler is planned for release in June 2018.

Using Red for writing dapps

The Red/C3 toolchain will be fully integrated, and consist of the following:

- *Compilers* for each blockchain VM bytecode, starting with an Ethereum compiler
- An automated *tests module*, to guarantee better contract testing and, thus, higher safety
- *High-performance blockchain VM simulators* for extensive and exhaustive testing
- A wrapper to a minimal local blockchain node infrastructure to simplify deployment
- A sandboxed I/O mode to enforce security on devices running dapps

The complete Red/C3 stack will be about 100x smaller than the web stack currently used for dapps (+- 1 MB compared to 120 MB). This compactness will make deployment of dapps much easier than it currently is with existing tools.

Among the first dapps to be built will be a Red wallet and a community chat.

Red's roadmap

What does the future bring for Red? Its roadmap can be found at `https://www.red-lang.org/p/roadmap.html` and in more detail at `https://trello.com/b/FlQ6pzdB/red-tasks-overview`.

After the 0.6.4. GUI console release, the main focus will be on the 0.7.0 release, which will provide full I/O and networking support, some features of which will certainly be needed in the Red/C3 toolchain. Android support is coming along well (for a demo, see `https://www.red-lang.org/2018/04/sneak-peek-at-red-on-android.html`), and is planned for the 0.7.1 release.

The next big milestones before the 1.0 release are as follows:

- **0.8**: Support for modules, to facilitate working on bigger and more complex Red projects
- **0.8.5**: Integrating an advanced garbage collector in the Red runtime
- **0.9**: Concurrency support, initially like coroutines, before evolving into a full-concurrent actor model

Another option is to declare 0.7.1 the last release before 1.0, moving major development portions to come after that release.

Red's toolchain is now still partly written in REBOL 2. Red will become truly self hosted when Red and its toolchain are completely rewritten in Red, which will also lead to faster compilation.

Some useful references

Red is still a young project, so its documentation lacks depth and examples. However, Red's popularity is growing rapidly, so this situation is expected to improve in the near future.

A number of documentation links can be found at `https://www.red-lang.org/p/documentation.html`, among which is the official Red documentation, also found at `https://doc.red-lang.org/` (which is still under construction).

The following websites can help you out when you need more examples or explanations:

- The Red By Example site (`http://www.red-by-example.org/index.html`), maintained by Arie Van Wingerden and Mike Parr
- The Red Beginners Reference Guide at `http://www.mycode4fun.co.uk`, maintained by Alan Brack
- Red documentation in the form of a Notebook at `http://helpin.red/`, by André Ungaretti
- The Red Programming site at `http://redprogramming.com/Home.html` by Nick Antonaccio

An ever-growing collection of links to articles on specific topics and discussions can be found on GitHub at `https://github.com/red/red/wiki`. I particularly recommend Gregg Irwin's Primer, which is found at `https://github.com/red/red/wiki/Primer`.

A growing collection of Red tools can be found at `https://github.com/rebolek/red-tools`. To explore concrete projects made in Red, visit `https://github.com/red/code/`.

If you have questions, ask them on Stack Overflow at `https://stackoverflow.com/questions/tagged/red`, or, for an even faster response, try Red's many Gitter channels at `https://gitter.im/red/home`.

Summary

In this chapter, you got a glimpse of some advanced features that Red has to offer. We saw how powerful reactive programming techniques make it possible to link two or more objects, so that if one changes, the others change with it. You got an introduction to Red/System, the lower layer of the Red platform, and learned how to incorporate its power to improve performance or to do low-level coding from within your Red apps. We captured command-line arguments for our script, and used `call` to start other programs. We learned how to use the `vector!`, `hash!`, and `map!` datatypes for performance when working with number series and dictionaries. At the end, you got a glimpse of the (near) future of Red's development, and you acquired a collection of the best links to turn to if you need more help.

We have now come to the end of our Red journey. I hope that this whirlwind overview has shown you why Red is a rising star in the software world, and I hope that you will start using it in your projects. See you in the Red universe!

Questions

1. Draw a 10 x 10 sized `base` face, and make it draggable with the `loose` facet. Add a text field that displays the `offset` of the box by using `react`, so that the text changes when the `base` is dragged.

2. A color of a face can be specified as `face/color: as-color r g b`, where r, g, and b are respectively the red, green, and blue content of the color (they are integers between 0 and 255). Alternatively, you can use `face/color/1` for red, and `/2` and `/3` for green and blue.
   Write a program that adjusts the color of a white base face, changing each of the r, g, b values by changing three sliders. If this works, then write a reactive version. Note how the reactive code is much simpler.

3. Examine the Red/System code in the `ch10/hello.reds` source file. Compile and execute it.

4. Write a Red/System function that prints in `Red/System`. Call this from a Red script that says `in Red` before and after the `include` of the Red/System code. Explain the output. If you use a `#system` block instead of `#system-global`, you can call the Red/System functions directly in it. Try this out.

5. Make a `map!` with string keys that only differ in case. Experiment with `select` and `put`, both with and without the `/case` refinement.

Further reading

The official documentation on Reactive programming can be found at `https://doc.red-lang.org/en/reactivity.html`.

You can find the detailed specification of Red/System at `https://static.red-lang.org/red-system-specs-light.html`.

Assessments

Chapter 1

1. Red/System is the part of Red needed to do lower-level programming like C.
2. A full-stack language is a language that can be used on the whole spectrum of programming, from systems level to high-level language construction. Red together with Red/System is able to do that.
3. Red and LISP both have the block (or list) as its basic structure, for code as well as for data.
4. 1) Red has a very small tool-chain, with no installation and configuration

    2) The size of its executables is around 1 Mb

    3) The reduced size of its source files.

5. A dialect is a specialized high-level language written in Red. Examples: parse, view, Red/C3
6. Red is compiled to native code, while REBOL is always interpreted.
7. Red runs in Windows, Linux, Android, OS X and FreeBSD environments in a 32 bit version, also on ARMv5 processors.

Chapter 2

1. Refer to `exercise1.red`

2. `red.r` is the REBOL script used currently to compile Red to Red/System, and Red/System to native code
3. A self-hosting language has a compiler that is written in itself (in the case of Red, written in Red)
4. The `do` function
5. `libRedRT` is not needed in release mode
6. The compiled code of `libRedRT` is contained within the program's executable
7. Visual Studio Code with the Red plugin gives you code completion

Chapter 3

1. It gives a *** **Script Error: John has no value.** Corrected: `name: "John"`
2. See explanation in text
3. `i1 ;== 1    i2  ;=`
   The point is that (`i1: 1`) itself has the value 1 and the effect that `i1` refers to 1 from then on.
4. `print [10 * 5] ;== 50`

   `probe [10 * 5]   ;== [10 * 5]`

5. `to_float 42` *** **Script Error: to_float has no value.**
   `to_float` is not a known word.

6. (`Chapter03/evaluation.red`):

   ```
   print (6 < 13) and (42 < 33)   ;== false
   print (43 < 42) xor (44 < 43)  ;== false
   print complement 3             ;== -4
   ```

7. `a: "red" ;== "red"`
   `b: copy a ;== "red"`
   `a = b ;== true ;same value`
   `a == b ;== true ;same value and datatype`
   `a =? b ;== false ;not the same object!`

8. `print [3 = 2 tab 5 = 5 tab 1 = 1.0]    ; == false    true`
   `true`
9. `on = (5 = 5) ;== true`
10. `? now`

    ```
    REFINEMENTS:

    /year => Returns year only.

    /month => Returns month only.

    /day => Returns day of the month only.

    /time => Returns time only.

    /zone => Returns time zone offset from UCT (GMT) only.

    /date => Returns date only.
    ```

```
/weekday => Returns day of the week as integer (Monday is day 1).

/yearday => Returns day of the year (Julian).

/precise => High precision time.
/utc => Universal time (no zone).
```

11. `square-root 9 + square-root 9`

Same as: `square-root (9 + square-root 9)`

Same as: `square-root (9 + 3)`

Same as: `square-root (12)   ;== 3.464101615137754`

`(square-root 9) + square-root 9     ;== 6.0`

12. `minimal.red`

```
-c compilation:  66kB
-r compilation:  583 kB
```

Chapter 4

1. see `testing-conditions.red` QA 1
2. `out  ;== "bad luck"`
3. see `raining.red`
4. see `testing_conditions.red`; QA 4
5. see `testing_conditions.red`; QA 5
6. see `repetitions.red`; QA 6
7. see `count-down.red`

Chapter 5

1. `data: ["A" "B" "C" "D"]` is a series of strings, the following is a series of characters: `data: [#"A" #"B" #"C" #"D"]`
2. see `navigating-and-looping.red` section ; moving to the tail.
3. see `navigating-and-looping.red` section ; back.
4. see `navigating-and-looping.red` section ; skip.
5. see `navigating-and-looping.red` ; QA 5.

6. see `getting-info.red` section ; selecting an item

7. see `getting-info.red` section ; QA 7

8. see `getting-info.red` section ; QA 8

9. see `getting-info.red` section ; QA 9

10. see `getting-info.red` ; QA 10

11. see `changing-series.red` ; QA 11

12. see `strings-as-series.red` ; QA 12

Chapter 6

1. see `do-error-runtime.red` for an explanation about the error and when you get to see it.

2. see `do-does-has-func.red` section ; QA 1

3. see `do-does-has-func.red` section ; QA 2 ?
   The variable `num` defined in `has1` becomes a global variable, whereas `has2` turns its `num2` argument into a local variable.

4. see `do-does-has-func.red` section ; QA 4

5. see `function-atrributes.red` section ; QA 5

6. see `function-atrributes.red` section ; QA 6

7. see `working-with-functions.red` section ; QA 7

8. see `working-with-functions.red` section ; QA 8
   Restricting the type of n with `n [integer!]` is also ok, but would provoke an exception.
   To test `if n = 0` you can also write `if zero? n`

9. see `working-with-functions.red` section ; QA 9

10. see `objects.red` ; QA 10

11. see `objects.red` QA 11

Chapter 7

1. see `reading-and-writing-files.red`, section QA 1: each item is written on a different line.

2. idem QA 2

3. idem QA 3

4. see `saving-and-loading.red` QA 4: after load the block structure is recovered.

5. see `saving-and-loading.red` QA 5

6. see `currency-rates3.red`

Chapter 8

1. see `bitsets.red` section QA 1
2. see `bitsets.red` section QA 2
3. see `bitsets.red` section QA 3
4. see `how-parse-works.red` section QA 4
5. see `how-parse-works.red` section QA 5
6. see `searching-and-changing.red` QA 6
7. see `searching-and-changing.red` QA 7
8. see `searching-and-changing.red` QA 8
9. see `searching-and-changing.red` QA 9
10. see `more-features.red` QA 10

Chapter 9

1. see `currency-rates-gui2.red`
2. see `faces-are-objects.red`
3. see `close-window-quit.red` and `close-window-unview.red`
4. see `container-layout.red` section QA 4
5. see `button-check.red`
6. see `sorted-text-list.red`
7. see `extracted-text-list.red`
8. see `text-hover-wheel.red`
9. see `drawing-lines.red`

Chapter 10

1. see `reactive-drag.red`

2. Non-reactive version is `box-color-non-reactive.red`, reactive version is `box-color-reactive.red`

3. see `hello.reds`

   ```
   Compile it with: red -r hello.reds
   To execute:     ./hello
   ```

4. `print-test.red` calls `print-test.reds`

5. see `perf-datatypes.red`, section QA 5

Other Books You May Enjoy

If you enjoyed this book, you may be interested in these other books by Packt:

Rust Programming By Example
Guillaume Gomez, Antoni Boucher

ISBN: 978-1-78839-063-7

- Compile and run the Rust projects using the Cargo-Rust Package manager
- Use Rust-SDL features such as the event loop, windows, infinite loops, pattern matching, and more
- Create a graphical interface using Gtk-rs and Rust-SDL
- Incorporate concurrency mechanism and multi-threading along with thread safety and locks
- Implement the FTP protocol using an Asynchronous I/O stack with the Tokio library

Rust Standard Library Cookbook
Jan Nils Ferner, Daniel Durante

ISBN: 978-1-78862-392-6

- How to use the basic modules of the library: strings, command line access, and more
- Implement collections and folding of collections using vectors, Deque, linked lists, and more
- Handle various file types, compressing and decompressing data
- Search for files with glob patterns
- Implement parsing through various formats such as CSV, TOML, and JSON
- Utilize drop trait, the Rust version of destructor
- Resource locking with Bilocks

Leave a review - let other readers know what you think

Please share your thoughts on this book with others by leaving a review on the site that you bought it from. If you purchased the book from Amazon, please leave us an honest review on this book's Amazon page. This is vital so that other potential readers can see and use your unbiased opinion to make purchasing decisions, we can understand what our customers think about our products, and our authors can see your feedback on the title that they have worked with Packt to create. It will only take a few minutes of your time, but is valuable to other potential customers, our authors, and Packt. Thank you!

Index